21 YEARS FREE...

EL PIANO

Bob Jackson & Magdalena Chávez

with

Alice Whiteley

Elaina Smith
Thushi Perera

plus input from

Mike Jackson
Miriam Perea
Raquel Raya
Florence

Almost all food photographs:
Bob and Elena Jackson with Alice Whiteley
Real food. No stylists. No enhancements.

Almost all people photographs:
Tom Greenly
Richard Greenly Photography
Thank you Tom.

Cover photograph and design - Bob and Elena Jackson
The Community Table
Over a period of 5 years, until there was no space left, customers paid £1 to borrow the
tools to each to carve their names.
In total the effort raised more than £1800 for charity.

About EL PIANO

A multi-award winning eatery, EL PIANO has long been a destination for a wide range of diners. The menu is wholly free from animal products, gluten, nuts, palm oil, and now refined sugar, so we attract a broad custom. People with eating restrictions eat with us regularly as well as ominvores, including carnivores. They say that the flavours are first rate, the ingredients high quality and that they know everything is made on site from primary ingredients, even the noodles.

Over the years we have added the cookschool, the B&B and a busy take-away, and in 2018 we move into our 21st year of trading in an industry that is notorious for failure. Focusing entirely on foods that, until recently, were considered to be for the faddish few, we have, by 'sticking to our knitting', managed to attract everyone from students to bankers, from the drug squad to the local chapter of AA.

Part of our attraction has undoubtedly been the coffee, freshly roasted, ground daily and brewed in a simple jug, strained and then frothily enjoyed. We hope it has also been due to the welcome EL PIANO extends to all who come and due to our neighbourhood where all these years we have been a part of street festivals and fund-raising.

In the early years we were also the latest opening premises in the city, operating until the heady hour of half past midnight under what was then known as a Late Night Refreshment House License. Without our late night custom of tea and coffee drinkers, largely from the then called 'gay community' we would not be here.

The support and kindness that we have been shown by people is a common theme of EL PIANO. We have had all sorts of help; advice from council officers and professionals, creative repairs from refrigeration engineers, plumbers, electricians and stonemasons, soft loans from friends, plus extended credit terms from suppliers. Then there have been the staff, many of whom have worked and worked and worked. Finally of course there is the family, thirteen of whom have put their shoulders to the wheel. All of these people have had the interests of EL PIANO at heart and recognised our commitment to more than commerce. Our success therefore belongs to many.

Compiling this cookbook gave us the opportunity to look back and remember some of the small steps that brought us here. The food is only part of it. We hope that you enjoy the recipes and also see past them to the spirit of the organisation that generated them.

*For our many
friends,
customers,
staff,
suppliers,
past and present,
who have supported
EL PIANO
all these years.*

We've learned loads from you.

Thank you.

index and table of contents combined

index and table of contents combined

Our approach...

Allergens
Recipes that contain any of the 14 official allergens are listed on page 220.

Chilli
Just like people, chillies come in all shapes, sizes and levels of punch. Often the smaller the chilli, the bigger the punch. Different colours have slightly different flavours – red for a sweeter heat and green for a more savoury one. For our kitchens, we use medium heat, long red chillies, as found in most supermarkets.

Coconut - see page 219

Flours & baking powder
While many of us are used to how wheat flour works, the ins and outs of the gluten free flours may be less familiar. A lot of these flours aren't mass produced, so they vary harvet to harvest AND they can all work in their own unique ways. Don't fret though - we have gone through many trials and errors to work out the best flours for each recipe (so you don't have to!). While we advise not swapping the flours around, you can swap buckwheat flour for maize flour in the cake recipes. Any recipe calling for baking powder assumes a gluten-free variety.

Herbs
Working in a commercial kitchen, we get so used to using regular sized 'bunches' from our veg merchant. We realize this doesn't apply to the home kitchen, so our reference to bunches is to the average sized bunch you get in your local supermarket – around 80g. Chopped, these usually make a good sized handful, but, as with everything in cooking, keep tasting as you add things.

Measurements & equipment
We have realised that some measuring systems do the job better than others. This has led us to mix our measuring methods - American cups, and also metric measures, litres(L) grams(g), millilitres(ml) as well as tablespoons(TBL) and teaspoons(tsp). Conversion rates between systems are available online. For our recipes we recommend buying a set of measuring cups and spoons, a calibrated jug and a set of electric scales so that you can move between systems with ease.

Mylks
In El Piano we try to secure the best quality products for our kitchen. The mylks we use in our recipes have minimal additives. Choose stabiliser and additive-free products or expect different results!

Numbers
Recipes, unless stated otherwise, are designed for 4 people of moderate appetite.

...things you should know

Ovens
It's impossible to know how your oven bakes as each oven has its own signature. Most recipes call for a medium heat. Simply choose the mid point on your dial.

Peeling
In our busy lives, time is precious, so here in our kitchen, we try to save as much time as possible. We ditched peeling veg long ago, so none of our recipes require it, not even ginger. There is the added bonus of all the goodness in the skin or peel...

Repeating ourselves
We think it's maddening to have to flip from page to page to complete a chosen dish. So rather than refer the cook to another page for, say, the sauce, some recipes are repeated, so that everything a cook needs to know about one dish appears together on the same page. The Burger on p.108 is the single exception to this.

Salt
A staple in nearly all kitchens yet, often a dirty word, salt is used liberally in our kitchen, bringing out the flavour of many dishes, both savoury and sweet. We state the salt level for our recipes, but feel free to change this. Keep trying your food and adjusting the salt to your taste.

Soy vs. soya
These words to refer to the same thing. Soy beans in the USA and soya in the UK.

Sweeteners - see page 219

Tofu
Tofu is like no other product. Similar to the flours we use, tofu can fluctuate in its appearance and texture. We use a very firm tofu for the savoury dishes and a softer, or silken, tofu for the deserts.

Vanilla
Ditching refined sugar was quite a challenge when we first made the decision, as we had to ditch many products, such as vanilla essence. We now use fresh vanilla pods whizzed finely. If you can't find this, and eliminating refined sugar is not an issue for you, vanilla essence will work, measure for measure.

Variation and freedom
No two mushrooms will ever be the same. While all the recipes have been tested, results vary each time. Try and enjoy the magic of food that has character. Our approach, while well informed by our knowledge of food chemistry, is very much about using what you have to hand and adapting recipes to what you like best.

1
Starters

Hannes homage

We came across this pâté in a tiny restaurant in El Segundo in California, owned by Chef Hannes. We have tried to recreate it here with all respect to the originator.

The beauty of this pâté is that it is a proportional recipe so you make as much or as little as you want...

All you will need is

> *cooked potatoes, either peeled and boiled, or*
> *baked, with the flesh scraped out, pressed into 2 cups*
> *1 cup of fresh basil, finely chopped*
> *salt and pepper to taste*
> *a drizzle of olive oil*

- Hand mash the potato together with the chopped basil.
- Add salt and pepper to taste.
- Serve topped with a drizzle of olive oil.

In the restaurant we serve both this and the hummus below with either toast or crudité. The truth is that hummus is probably better with the raw vegetable sticks and the hannas homage is better with toast.

Hummus

Rich in calcium and almost endlessly variable, this vegan staple is quick and inexpensive to make. Add parsely, beetroot, carmelised onions, chipotle sauce to hummus for variation, but beware: this will reduce its shelf life. By all means cook chickpeas from dried but it's a much longer process.

All you will need is

> *1 x 400g tin/can of chickpeas*
> *3 TBL sesame paste aka tahini*
> *water*
> *2-3 cloves fresh garlic*
> *juice of 1 lemon*
> *1 tsp salt*

- Drain the chick peas and dump them in a bowl.
- Add the tahini.
- Separately whizz the lemon juice, garlic and salt, mincing the garlic well, to avoid surprise chunks!
- Pour into the bowl with the chickpeas and whizz, adding water and salt until the hummus is to your desired consistency and taste.

Pease pudding

Pease pudding hot
Pease pudding cold
Pease pudding in
the pot
9 days old.

Perhaps the fastest soup ever...

> *2 cups of frozen peas*
> *½ diced white onion*
> *3 TBL extra virgin olive oil*
> *1½ cups of water*
> *1 tsp salt*
> *¼ tsp black pepper*

- Sauté everything in the oil except the salt and water..
- Add the water, cover and leave to simmer.
- After 20 minutes remove from the heat and whizz.
- Stir in the salt and pepper. Serve.

This is a really versatile soup because it is thick and hearty when hot, but solidifies once cold. Then it makes a great spread for crackers and sandwiches.

Lawrence's dip

This dip was a great favourite in Alice's house. Her Dad used to make it and fill everyone up before the meal was served.

His main goal was to increase the amount of garlic they all ate!

Fast and inexpensive to make....

> 200ml soya milk
> 400ml sunflower oil
> 2 tsp lemon juice
> 2-5 tsp salt
> 4 tsp smoked paprika
> 2 grated cloves of garlic

- Whizz all ingredients together.
- Adjust seasonings to taste.
- Serve topped with a drizzle of olive oil.

Raw mushroom pâtê

This recipe makes use of the much under-used juniper berry which, when combined with a drop of brandy, provides the special flavour for a wonderful treat. Swap out the basil and/or the juniper for something you like better. Like so many of the EL PIANO recipes this is easy to adapt and make it your own.

All you will need is

> 500g mushrooms - any variety will do
> 1 TBL brandy
> 2 TBL any mylk
> barely a clove of fresh garlic
> 8 basil leaves
> 8 juniper berries
> 1 tsp salt

- Whizz the lot, refrigerate an hour or more, and serve.

In the restaurant we serve both of these with thinly sliced breads.

Miso soup

No cookbook is complete without miso soup.

1 TBL sunflower oil
½ onion, sliced in thin circles
½ carrot, thinly sliced in coins or match sticks
100g chopped pak choy is ideal, but really any crisp cabbage will do
1L water
4 TBL any miso
1 finely chopped spring onion to garnish

- Sauté the onions and the carrots in the oil until tender.
- Add the water and bring to the boil.
- Remove from the heat and stir in the miso.
- Throw on the chopped greens.
- Cover until the greens are wilted.
- Serve.

Thai-style yam broth

Quick! This soup can as easily be made with parsnips, or a combination of carrot, parsnip and potato.

1 fresh red chilli
1 TBL grated ginger (don't bother to peel it)
1 K chopped unpeeled orange yams/sweet potatoes
1L stock or water
100g creamed coconut (half a block)
1 stick of lemon grass and 4 lime leaves
Juice of ½ lime
4 tsp salt
3 TBL sunflower oil

- Sauté everything in the oil except the coconut and water.
- When the potatoes soften, add the water and coconut.
- Hook out the lemon grass and the lime leaves.
- Whizz and then check for salt before adding the lime juice.

Leftover spirals

To extract pomegranate seeds quickly, roll the pomegranate on a surface and listen and feel as the seeds inside loosen.

Cut the pomegranate in half. Invert each half over a bowl and bash with the back of a large spoon or rolling pin. The seeds just pop out!

Thank you Miranda.

This dish is all about the look. You can wrap the aubergines around almost anything, even chopped dates and grated apples. The key to the stunning presentation is the skewer through the centre and the jewels of pomegranate seeds dotted over the top.

All you will need is

> 1 aubergine per person served
> mashed savoury leftovers
> wooden skewers or toothpicks
> fresh pomegranate and pomegrate syrup (optional)
> extra virgin olive oil and salt

- Slice aubergines lengthways and salt to reduce the moisture.
- Wring out the aubergine slices.
- Shallow fry them flat in olive oil.
- Form the mashed leftovers into sausage shapes and wrap the aubergine around them, skewering them to hold them together.
- Arrange on a plate and dot with pomegranate seeds and an optional drizzle of pomegranate syrup.

Sweet potato mousse

Easy to make and a great favourite with children, maybe because it's bright orange!

All you will need is

> 250-350g orange sweet potatoes
> 2 TBL lemon juice
> 50ml pure soya mylk - no flavourings or additives
> 100ml sunflower oil
> ¼ chopped, peeled onions
> ½ tsp salt

- Roast the potatoes in a medium oven until soft - about 20 minutes. Remove, cool and remove the skins.
- Whizz the soya mylk continuously, adding the oil steadily. It will thicken as the last of the oil goes in. Add the lemon juice.
- Now whizz with the potatoes and onion.
- Add the salt and serve.

Rich red potage

Lentils are a natural thickener and can be used to give body to any soup. Split red lentils are in fact peeled lentils, which, without their peel, and because they then fall into two halves, cook really quickly.

1K fresh tomatoes
3 TBL extra virgin olive oil
1 chopped white onion
3 TBL tomato paste
200g split red lentils
200ml water
1 TBL syrup (optional - a cure for rubbish tomatoes)
1 TBL salt

- Gently cook the tomatoes and onions in the oil, under a lid to keep in the flavour and moisture.
- Once the tomatoes and onions have broken up and become a wet stew (about 15-20 minutes), add the tomato paste, syrup, water and lentils.
- Cook gently, and covered, until the lentils disappear, about 20 minutes.
- Add the salt.

Leek & potato soup

An equal amount of chopped potatoes and leeks is the key to the flavour of this simple but perennial favourite.

1 K chopped potatoes
1 K fresh, stiff, chopped leeks - use them ALL (bar the roots)
1500ml stock or water
6 TBL extra virgin olive oil
1½ TBL salt
3 sage leaves or a sprig of rosemary, but not both

- Sauté the potatoes and leeks in the olive oil with the salt. (To wash leeks easily under the tap and remove any grit without them all falling apart, cut them lengthways, stopping just short of the root.)
- Add the herbs and the stock or water.
- Cook until the potatoes break up. The option then is to whizz or leave chunky.

Guacamolé

A trick from Bob's mother: an open avocado half will not go brown if unused and left in the fridge. Simply run it under the tap before stashing it.

Don't add olive oil to guacamolé. It's oily enough!

This is a family favourite and we make it for almost all our social gatherings.

All you will need is

> 2 ripe (soft) avocados per person served
> the juice of ½ lemon per avocado (others only use lime!)
> 1 large chopped tomato or equivalent cherry tomatoes per 2 avocados
> ½ tsp salt

- Open the avocado and spoon out the flesh.
- Mash all the ingredients together with bare hands and serve.

Tempura

Rice flour batter makes a light, almost indiscernable outer crust. Using corn flour results in a thicker shell. You choose.

All you will need is

> 100g rice flour or corn flour
> 150g sliced season vegetables
> 150ml ginger beer or ordinary beer
> sunflower oil

- Choose a deep enough pan for heating sufficient oil to deep fry the tempura.
- Mix the flour and fluid in a bowl
- Hand dip the veg in the mix.
- Place in the hot oil and remove when golden.
- Serve with a side dish of dipping sauce, 1 part tamari mixed with 1 part water, 1 part coconut sugar topped with grated ginger.

Samosas

Here's the skin. Halve it.

Find the centre of the curved edge. Fold upwards and apply the 'glue'.

Now the second flap, creating 2 'ears'.

Turn the pocket in your hand, with 'ears' at the back.

Now you have a pocket to stuff.

Fold and 'glue' the 'ears', pinching all the corners to seal.

Magdalena swears she will never forget the first time her friend Miranda made her eat a samosa. She still speaks of it as a defining moment in her culinary life.

To make the gluten-free skins:

> *1 cup buckwheat flour*
> *2 cups water*

- *Mix in a jug until smooth.*
- *Dab a few dots of light oil on a non-stick frying pan or crêpe pan until the air above the pan shimmers.*
- *Lift the pan from the heat. Pour on just enough mix to cover the pan base by rotating the pan so as to spread the mix as thinly as possible. If you over do it, tip excess back into the jug.*
- *When the edges are dry begin to loosen the thin skin with a spatula. Turn to cook the other side, less than a minute.*

To make the filling:

> *250g of cubed potatoes - no need to peel them*
> *100g cubed carrots - no need to peel them*
> *50g frozen peas*
> *½ cubed onion*
> *1 TBL curry powder and ½ TBL fennel or cumin seeds*
> *2 stems and the leaves of fresh coriander*
> *1 TBL salt*

- *Boil the carrots and potatoes until fully cooked.*
- *Remove from the heat and add the frozen peas and onion.*
- *Leave 10 minutes, then drain.*
- *Add the spices, herbs and salt.*

To fold and fry:

Follow the illustrations in the side-bar using a 'glue' of 2 TBL buckwheat flour and 2 TBL water, making more if needed. Wherever there are cracks, 'bandage' them with the glue. Fry in sunflower oil and remove when golden. Remember, however misshapen they may be, they will taste amazing.

Cream of mushroom

It's always a good idea with mushrooms to play down everything else so that their subtle flavour shines through.

Basil is an optional extra here, and even a touch of garlic, but it needs to be with a light hand.

Choose any mushrooms. Field mushrooms give a dark result, button mushrooms a lighter one and woodland mushrooms give an autumnal gold.

> 1K mushrooms
> 8 TBL extra virgin olive oil
> 4 TBL buckwheat flour
> 1L any mylk
> 4 tsp each of salt,
> pepper and a pinch of mustard powder are optional

- Gently cook the mushrooms (saves time not to cut them) and salt in the olive oil under a lid to keep in moisture. You don't want them to crisp up.
- Remove from the heat and add the flour.
- Return to the heat and add the fluid, stirring continously until thickened, about 15 minutes.
- Whizz with discretion, leaving some chunks of mushroom.

Corn chowder

Unusally 2 pans are needed for this thick and warming chowder.

> 1 x 400g tin sweet corn kernels, drained
> 500g cubed potatoes
> 500ml any mylk
> 1L stock or water (200ml white wine is an optional part of the fluid)
> 6 TBL extra virgin olive oil
> 4 TBL buckwheat flour
> 1 diced white onion
> 1 good sized sprig of sage and 1½ TBL salt

- Boil the potatoes, corn and the sage in half the fluid until the potatoes are fully cooked and disintegrating.
- Separately fry the onions in the oil until soft but not brown.
- Remove from the heat and stir in the flour until fully coated.
- Return to the heat and add the remaining fluids.
- Cook until thickened, stirring constantly, about 15 minutes.
- Add the potatoes, sage, corn and remaining fluid.
- Whizz, leaving some kernals for texture. Salt and serve.

Babaganoush

It used to be the case that aubergines were salted to neutralise their bitterness. Most varieties now, the bitterness has been bred out.

Babaganoush will solidify in the fridge. The flavours benefit from time to mingle.

The most delicate of pâtés, the trick here is not to over season it.

All you will need is

> *1 aubergine per person served - an average aubergine weighs around 200-250g*
> *1 tsp sesame paste aka tahini per aubergine*
> *¼ tsp cumin seeds (preferred) or ground cumin*
> *1 tsp lemon juice and ¼ tsp salt to taste*

- Roast the aubergines or blacken them on the barbeque or gas flame.
- Add the rest of the ingredients and whizz.
- Chill and serve.

Mud mushrooms

We used to make this recipe as part of the cookery demos in book shops all over the UK (yes...book shops!). The reason we chose to do this one is that it is so easy and so fast, needs no water (since book shops often lack a ready supply!), can be eaten off of a toothpick and the punters were always delighted. Mushrooms sweat fluid naturally (the only vegetable that loses weight on the shelf making it a headache for retailers to sell pre-packed!). The salt exacerbates this, and mixed with the darkening frying spices, creates the mud. In our cookschool a great favourite with children is the mud mushrooms. They seem to like the name, the speed with which it can be made and the savoury flavour.

All you will need is

> *280g whole button mushrooms*
> *4 TBL extra virgin olive oil*
> *4 tsp ground cumin*
> *3 tsp salt*

- Oil a frying pan lightly and heat until the air shimmers above the pan.
- Throw in the mushrooms, salt and spice.
- Fry until the mushrooms are tender.
- Serve.

2
Breads

Yeasted bread

If you have made bread using wheat you will find this mix to be much wetter. Because of this it is difficult to make a loaf that will cook all the way through so we recommend baking rolls instead.

Yeast needs sweetener, to be moist and kept warm. It emits gases which form air pockets.

The growing yeast makes the dough almost double in size. When it goes into the oven the shock of the heat kills the yeast, but the airpockets are 'fossilised' in bread and make it spongy.

Pre-heat the oven to medium-hot. Set away a pan of water to boil. Oil an oven tray. You will need:

> 200g maize flour, finely milled corn, not polenta
> 170g of chickpea flour aka gram, besan or garbanzo
> 1 TBL xanthum gum and 1 tsp salt
> 100ml sunflower oil and 50ml syrup
> ¼ cup of dried mixed herbs
> 1½ TBL dried yeast
> 200ml boiling water mixed with 150ml cold water
> 1-2 cups of polenta for rolling the dough

- Clear a surface for turning out the dough.
- Put all of the dry ingredients, except the polenta, in a bowl.
- Run your hands through the ingredients to eliminate lumps.
- Combine the oil and syrup in a jug, the water in another.
- Add the contents of both jugs to the bowl and mix well.
- Turn the mix out onto the polenta, sprinkled onto a clean surface. The purpose of the polenta is coat the outside.
- Roll the dough into a long sausage shape.
- Cut into medallions and turn them in the polenta.
- Place each on the oiled tray.
- Leave the tray over the boiling water, covered in a tea towel.
- When the rolls have increased in size, about 10 minutes, slide the tray into the oven for 15-20 minutes or until golden.
- Remove, ideally cool on a rack. Serve.

Crumpets

Metal crumpet rings are better than silicone as they conduct heat...

> 1 cup buckwheat flour
> 2 TBL coconut sugar and ¼ tsp salt
> 1 TBL dried yeast
> 225ml hot water mixed with 175 cold

- Mix everything together and let it stand around 5 minutes.
- Oil a large frying pan, sufficient for 6 crumpet rings.
- Put on a low heat. Divide the mix between 6 rings.
- The crumpets are done when bubbles appear, pop and dry out leaving holes across the surfaces.

Crêpes, blinis & pancakes

The vast majority of product mixes for pancakes sold in packets are virtually inedible and always expensive.

400g of buckwheat flour, mixed merely with water, will yield 20 wafer thin French-style crêpes or 80 Russian-style blinis - a wonderful gluten-free toast, bread or cracker for pâté.

If you put too much mix in the pan, and it seems too thick, just pour it off, back into the jug. It won't be long before you get the hang of it and a few thick ones to start with won't be enjoyed any the less.

All of these, crêpes, pancakes and blinis, can be frozen. The crêpes easily double as gluten-free wraps as well as cannelloni shells since they are so flexible.

All you need for crêpes and blinis is

> buckwheat flour
> water
> oil for the pan

For the American-style pancakes you will also need

> baking powder

To make the French-style crêpes:

- *Mix in a jug until smooth, 1 cup of buckwheat flour and 2 cups of water with ¼ tsp of salt.*
- *Heat a non-stick frying pan or crêpe pan to super hot.*
- *Oil the pan enough to ease any stick. Pour off any excess.*
- *Remove the pan from the heat. Pour the pancake mix onto the pan, rotating it so the mix thinly covers it.*
- *Return to the heat. When the edges come away easily, ease it off the pan with a spatula. Turn and cook a further 30 seconds.*
- *Slide onto a plate.*

To make American-style pancakes:

- *Mix in a jug until smooth, 1 cup of buckwheat flour and 1 cup of water with ¼ tsp of salt and 1 tsp baking powder.*
- *Heat a non-stick frying pan or crêpe pan to super hot.*
- *Oil the pan and spoon the mix on in circles.*
- *Cook until bubbles appear and then turn, cook and remove.*

To make blinis (an unyeasted version)

- *You will need crumpet rings or silicon rings.*
- *Create a mix that is somewhere between the two above, 1 cup of buckwheat flour and 1½ cups of water.*
- *Oil the rings and a non-stick pan. Pour the mix into the rings, choosing your thickness. Turn until both sides are cooked through. Fatter ones will toast!*

These recipes are open to many the variations. Sweet crêpes are great with added vanilla and spices. For a savoury version use finely diced onion, herbs and seeds. Nutritional yeast is fantastic in the batter. American-style pancakes are great with fresh fruit in the batter.

Corn bread

Bob's grandfather drove cattle west to the stockyards in Kansas City, a journey on horseback of around 3 weeks. In the mornings, the bacon was cooked in the cast iron skillet, afterwards, in went the gritty corn mix, to soak up the lard...

This is essentially a stiff batter, now baked in the oven with lashings of olive oil. Pre-heat the oven to medium heat and oil the oven tray generously with the olive oil.

> 1K corn meal aka polenta
> 250ml sunflower or similar light salad oil
> 2 tsp baking powder
> 3 TBL coconut sugar
> 1 TBL salt
> 1 L boiling water

- Mix all the dry ingredients in a bowl.
- Add the oil and work it through the flour by hand.
- Add the boiling water.
- Stir well and pour into an oven tray, oiled with olive oil.
- Bake for 20-30 minutes, or until the cornbread is solid.
- Cut into squares and serve.

Soft corn tortillas

Masa harina is a flour made from corn kernals soaked in lime, (the chemical, not the fruit) then rinsed, ground and dried.

> 2 cups of masa harina and extra for rolling out
> 1½ cups tepid water and 1 tsp salt

- Mix the ingredients together in a bowl and cover.
- After 30 minutes divide the dough into 15-20 equal balls.
- Heat a frying pan to medium heat.
- Roll out the balls into circles on the extra flour.
- Place them in the pan, turning four times within 30 seconds.
- Remove and keep warm in a cloth.

Corn chips

- Cut tacos into strips or pie shapes.
- Fry in sunflower oil.
- Salt and serve.

3
Fritters

Sushi frito

Sushi frito is the best thing ever.

This is an EL PIANO creation, combining the food value of seaweed, rice and tamari with the flavours of Japan.

The soak sauce is:

> 200g tamari with 200g water
> 1 bunch diced spring onions/scallions
> 20g grated ginger

- *Combine the ingredients for the soak sauce and set aside.*

For the balls:

> 500g cooked rice (about 175g uncooked rice)
> 250g grated courgettes
> 4 tsp grated ginger
> 50g chopped, pre-soaked seaweed
> 100g rice flour
> Sunflower oil or similar (not olive oil!) for frying

- *Combine the ingredients for the balls, except the oil, adding the flour last.*
- *Form into balls, fry in hot sunflower oil.*
- *Remove when brown and dump immediately into the soak sauce. Drain once fully drenched. Serve.*

Corn fritters

Stellar...

> 1 x 400g sweet corn, drained and whizzed
> 1-2 diced fresh red chillies, you choose your heat
> 80g chopped fresh coriander
> ½ diced white onion (optional)
> 1½ tsp salt
> 100g rice flour plus a bit extra if needed
> Sunflower oil or similar (not olive oil!) for frying

- *Put everything except the flour and the oil in a bowl.*
- *Add the flour, only enough to hold it together in the fryer. If they don't hold together, add a touch more flour...*
- *Wet hands. Form patties.*
- *Fry until golden. Serve.*

Mushroom & garlic patties

Mushrooms lose weight, as is mentioned a few times in this book... Very quickly what was a pile of fresh firm mushrooms descends, literally, into soft mush. This makes prescribing the weight of flour needed quite difficult. Go easy... only add more flour if the patties disintegrate in the fryer.

1K sliced fresh firm mushrooms
10-15g grated or minced fresh garlic
2½ tsp salt
Rice flour as required (!)
Sunflower oil or similar (not olive oil!) for frying

- Leave the mushrooms, garlic and salt in bowl.
- The amount of flour needed will depend on how long the mushrooms are left to sweat. Squeeze out the excess liquid before adding the flour. Add only enough flour just to bind it all. Once your hands are wet, so the patties don't stick to them, you will find that much less flour is needed than you think.
- Place the patties in hot sunflower oil.
- Remove when evenly golden and serve.

Pestolitos

An absolute corker of a fritter...keep the flour to the bare minimum. The mix is whizzed so no careful chopping is needed.

4 cups of chopped fresh spinach
4 cups of hacked up mushrooms
4 cups of coarsely chopped fresh basil
4 cups of quartered fresh tomatoes
1 TBL salt
Sunflower oil or similar (not olive oil!) for frying

- Put everything except the flour and the oil in a bowl.
- Whizz it to the desired texture. In EL PIANO we leave it fairly coarse.
- Add the flour.
- Wet hands. Form into patties and fry in hot sunflower oil removing when evenly golden. Serve.

Scrambled scotch egg

Things don't stick to
wet hands...

Thanks to Adam Wilson for this great idea!

For the outer shell you will need:
> 1 chopped onion
> 50ml sunflower oil
> 1 cup textured soya mince (TVP)
> 2 cups of water
> 1 tsp salt
> 2 tsp black pepper
> 1 TBL mixed herbs
> ½ cup chickpea flour and some more if required

- Fry the onion in the oil.
- Add the TVP. Stir so that it absorbs the oil yet does not burn.
- Add the water and herbs, cover and cook on a low heat, checking periodically to ensure it has not simmered dry.
- When the water is absorbed, the TVP uniformly soft, about 20-30 minutes, remove from the heat and add the salt.
- Stir in the chickpea flour, enough to glue the mix together but not so much as to make it pasty.
- Form the mix into 'golf ball' sized spheres. Set aside.

For the inside you will need:
> 300g tofu
> 1 TBL sunflower oil
> 150ml soya mylk
> ¼ cup of nutritional yeast
> 1 tsp salt

- Heat the oil in a frying pan and crumb the tofu into the oil.
- Add the mylk, salt and nutritional yeast, stirring constantly.
- When the tofu is at the preferred texture and dryness, remove from the heat.

Make the 'egg':

- Take one of the 'golf balls'. Flatten it into a patty. Set aside.
- Take a second 'golf ball'. Flatten it into a patty in your hand.
- Place a large marble sized sphere of the tofu mix in the middle of the patty and cover with the first patty, sealing the sides and ultimately rolling it into a ball.
- Deep fry in sunflower oil until golden brown.

50

Curried banana fritters

Fritters can be par-fried, then frozen. Use directly from the freezer. Finish them off in a medium-low oven

1. No-one is bent over the fryer in their ball-gown in the final moments before any guests arrive.

2. This reduces the fat ingested. As they crisp up they shed some of the original frying oil.

This rather strange combination is a long term favourite in the restaurant and has appeared on more than one menu. As with all of our fritters, if you are not going to fry them all at once, it is best to leave the flour out and then add it, fritter by fritter, just before frying.

1K boiled potatoes
6 ripe bananas
3 TBL curry powder
1 TBL salt
5 TBL chickpea flour aka besan, gram or garbanzo bean flour
Sunflower oil or similar (not olive oil!) for frying

- *Smash the cooked potatoes by hand with the bananas.*
- *Add the flour, salt and spices.*
- *Roll into lozenge shapes and fry in hot sunflower oil removing when evenly golden.*
- *Serve.*

Pineapple fritters

All you will need is:

1 fresh pineapple, peeled and sliced in half moons
2 TBL curry powder
1 TBL salt
200g chickpea flour aka besan, gram or garbanzo bean flour
250ml water
Sunflower oil or similar (not olive oil!) for frying

- *Mix the flour with the water, salt and spices.*
- *Dip the sliced pineapple in the batter and then place in the hot sunflower oil.*
- *Remove when evenly golden.*
- *Serve.*

Tinas

Mayra Salazar, from La Paz, was the main cook in EL PIANO Granada from 2007 - 2011. She shared with us her mother Cristina's dish, with no name of its own. So we named it Tina after her mum. These fritters have been among the most enduring favourites of EL PIANO .

All you will need is

> 800g of grated carrots
> 800g of chopped leeks or spring onions
> 2 TBL salt
> 1 cup of syrup
> 5-10 TBL rice flour
> Sunflower oil or similar (not olive oil!) for frying

- Mix the vegetables with the salt.
- Leave them for 10-15 minutes to sweat out moisture.
- Squeeze them out and discard the salty 'water'.
- Mix with scant flour. Press into patties with wet hands.
- Fry in hot sunflower oil. If they disintegrate then you need
 more flour. Remove when evenly golden. Serve.

Neeps

Europe has many root crops, often inexpensive when in season. Grating any of them, and adding whatever flavours you like, is an excellent way to arrive at your family favourite. Good choices are carrots, celariac, potatoes, turnips, parsnip, swede. Avoid 'wet' veg like squash that need more flour which in turn soaks up more grease. Parsnips are a peculiarly British vegetable. This is a popular use of this sweet and buttery vegetable.

> 800g of grated parsnips
> 1 cup of chopped fresh corander
> 2 fresh minced chillies
> 1 TBL salt
> 5 TBL rice flour
> Sunflower oil or similar (not olive oil!) for frying

- Mix the vegetables with the salt and leave them to sweat.
- Squeeze them out and discard the salty 'water'.
- Mix with scant flour. Press them into patties with wet hands.
- Fry in hot sunflower oil and remove when evenly golden.
- Serve.

Bhajis

This staple British fare is only onions, whereas the pakoras below traditionally contain vegetables and no onions at all.

These are amazing hot or cold and are fantastic travelling snacks. Make sure you pack them in paper to absorb any excess oil.

Consider a small pile of chopped onions and an equally sized pile of flour. Drop oil on to each of the piles. It will slide off the onions and be sucked up by the flour. The variety in the type of bhajis is all about the flour. More onion in the mix, more lacy the result and less grease into the mouth. Conversely, less onion, more flour and the result is cakey and far more fatty.

For lacy bhajis you will need

> 1K of finely sliced white onions
> 1 cup chickpea flour, aka besan, gram or garbanzo bean flour
> 4 TBL curry powder (we use Madras)
> 1½ TBL salt
> Sunflower oil or similar (not olive oil!) for frying

- Salt the onions and leave them for 10-15 minutes. They will sweat out moisture.
- Squeeze out the onions and discard the salty 'water'.
- Add the spices and mix with scant flour.
- Form into patties with wet hands and deep or shallow fry until golden brown.

Pakoras

All you will need is

> 200g sliced potato
> 200g chopped carrot
> 100g frozen peas
> 20g chopped fresh coriander
> 1 TBL salt
> 3 TBL curry powder (we use Madras)
> 1 cup chickpea flour, aka besan, gram or garbanzo bean flour
> ¾ cup water
> Sunflower oil or similar (not olive oil!) for frying

- Mix the water with the flour, the spices and salt.
- Add the vegetables.
- Drop the mix by spoonfuls into hot oil. Remove when evenly golden. Serve.

Falafels

Our falafels might never have been free of the floury, dry taste often associated with falafels but for a British pensioner. He had spent his childhood in the Lebanon. "Use loads of parsely, far more than you think. The fresh green steams in the mix and keeps them moist."

Charles is right.

The shape of a falafel varies world wide, but all contain chick peas...

You will need

> 400g tin/can chick peas, drained
> 1 finely chopped white onion
> 4-5 finely chopped, or grated, cloves of garlic
> 50g chickpea flour, aka besan, gram or garbanzo bean flour
> 2 cups chopped fresh parsley and 1 tsp salt
> Sunflower oil or similar (not olive oil!) for frying

- Smash the chickpeas by hand or with a potato masher for a full-bodied, textured result - whizz them for an even, pasty texture (easy to see our preference!!)
- Add the rest of the ingredients.
- Mould into balls or flat patties, fry until golden and serve.

Sweet potato fritters

This is a falafel with a slight nod to Persian cuisine and can as easily be made with chickpea flour, aka besan, gram or garbanzo bean flour. A further variation is to add diced onions.

All you will need is

> 1K sweet potatoes or yams
> 80g of chopped fresh corander
> 1 tsp salt and ½ tsp ground cumin
> 3 TBL rice flour
> Sunflower oil or similar (not olive oil!) for frying

- Grate the sweet potato.
- Add the herbs, spices and salt.
- Set it aside and wait just 10 minutes as the salt and spices draw out the moisture in the potatoes.
- Wet your hands and then mix with scant flour.
- Press into balls or patties and shallow or deep fry. Serve.

4
Salads

Baked red cabbage

For all that it's brightly coloured and flexible like plastic, silicone is a form of glass, made from silica, (sand) and not from petro-chemicals. Like glass it's heat resistant withstanding up to 500°F. Little sticks to it so time spent oiling trays and tins is reduced and it's easy to clean.

All you will need is

> ½ coarsely cut red cabbage
> 4 sliced red apples
> ½ cup of raisins
> 1 stick of cinnamon
> ¼ cup of cider vinegar, white wine vinegar is also fine
> 1 tsp salt

- Combine everything and tip onto an oven tray.
- Cover, ideally with a silicone baking sheet to keep in the moisture. Tin foil is workable but is thrown away and made from aluminium.
- Bake for 30-45 minutes The cabbage is ready when soft.
- Can be served hot or cold.

Smoked sauerkraut

This dish really lives up to its name.

> 2 cups finely chopped white cabbage
> ¼ tsp salt
> 1 TBL coconut sugar
> 1 tsp liquid smoke

- Combine, leave to stand 10 minutes and eat!

Beetroot sauerkraut

Beetroot, another underused vegetable...

> 2 cups grated fresh beetroot
> 3 crushed juniper berries
> 1 clove of minced garlic
> 2 TBL coconut sugar
> 1 TBL white wine vinegar
> ¼ tsp salt

- Combine, leave to stand 10 minutes and eat!

Kasha salad

Buckwheat is herbacious and, for many customers, easier to digest. Believed to be indiginous to the Russian steppes, buckwheat later appeared on the plains of the USA. This has lent some weight to the idea that the Native Americans came from Russia. Some people won't like that idea... Probably fake news...

You will need:

> *1 cup of buckwheat grain*
> *½ cup of raisins*
> *the seeds of ½ a pomegranate*
> *zest of ½ an orange*
> *½ cup of chopped fresh parsley*

- Cook the buckwheat grain in 2 cups of water until the grain is soft, about 20 minutes, adding more water if necessary.
- Discard any excess water.
- Add the raisins while the grain is still warm so that they might plump up a little.
- When the mix has cooled add the parsley and orange zest.
- **Now the pomegranate seeds. To extract pomegrate seeds quickly, roll the pomegranate on a surface. Listen and feel as the seeds inside loosen. Cut the pomegranate in half. Invert each half over a bowl and bash with the back of a large spoon or rolling pin. The seeds just pop out!**
- Toss and serve.

Bean salad

> *3 x 400g drained beans of different colours*
> *1 diced red pepper*
> *½ cup of chopped parsley*
> *1 minced clove of fresh garlic - just a hint - don't over do it*
> *30ml olive oil*
> *¼ tsp salt*
> *½ tsp black pepper*
> *juice of 1 lemon*

- *Combine everything and check for flavours, adjusting to your taste.*
- *Serve!*

Jade salad

The aim of preparing naked orange segments is to leave behind the peel, the pith and the membrane within the orange itself. All that is left are the tiny little orange sacs full of juice.

If you are uncertain how to do it, there are full instructions on p.102.

This is an adaptation of an oriental salad, originally full of sea insects, and first introduced to EL PIANO from family who had adapted it from Hugh Carpenter - all of which goes to show that most everything we do in the kitchen we learn from other cooks... Jade salad is remarkable for the vibrancy of the colours. The deep green of the spinach contrasts with the red, making it a great seasonal favourite.

100g sliced, firm, white button mushrooms (optional)
500g washed, chopped fresh spinach
1 bunch washed, diced, spring onions/scallions (optional)
1 thinly sliced red pepper
zest of 1 orange
the naked orange segments of 2 oranges
50ml sunflower oil
20ml rice vinegar
30ml syrup
10g grated ginger

- Combine the oil, vinegar, syrup and ginger in a jug. Set aside.
- Combine everything else in a salad bowl.
- Just before serving, dress the salad.
- Serve.

Mushroom & basil salad

Easy. A great favourite with EL PIANO with cooks because it is so fast to make...

500g sliced, firm, white button mushrooms
⅓ chopped fresh basil
100ml extra virgin olive oil
30ml best balsamic vinegar
½ tsp salt

- Combine. Oil first, before the salt or vinegar. The oil protects the mushrooms from the salt and acid so that they stay firmer for longer.
- Serve.

Japan cup

Seaweed is a source of iron and minerals and has a taste reminiscent of the sea.

Extremely simple...

You will need:

> *1 finely sliced cucumber or, more chunky if you prefer*
> *8 pieces of dried wakame*
> *2 TBL sesame oil - toasted is ideal*
> *2 TBL of rice vinegar*

- Soak the wakame in hot water 5-10 minutes until it is soft.
- Drain and shred by hand or chop finely.
- Combine everything and serve.

Andalus salad

Extremely simple, very rich... and surprisingly delicious.

You will need:

> *2 oranges cut into naked orange segments. If this is new to you, please see p.102 for a full explanation.*
> *½ cup of black stoned olives*
> *½ cup of chopped dates*
> *chopped parsely for garnish (optional)*

- Combine everything and serve.

Waldorf salad

Using this as a base, go off on a taste adventure...

...ginger, tamari, oil and spring onion

...sundried tomatoes, olive oil and sesame seeds...

...curry mayo and raisins...

...make it your own...

Based on the classic salad created at the Waldorf Hotel in New York (before Astoria got in there...) If there is a secret, it is to chop everything the same size.

You will need:

> 200g chopped celery
> 200g chopped eating apples
> 80g chopped dates
> 50g toasted, salted broad beans aka habas fritas
> ½ cup of untreated, additive free soya mylk
> 1½ cups of sunflower oil
> 1 tsp coconut sugar
> ¼ tsp salt and 1 TBL lemon juice

- Put the the celery, apples, dates and broad beans in a bowl.
- Whizz the soya mylk and add the sunflower oil bit by bit to make the mayonnaise, adding the salt, lemon juice and coconut sugar at the end. More on mayo see p.158.
- Throw it over the celery mix, toss and serve.

Blanched greens

Any greens will do, although spinach reduces a bit too much. Spring cabbage, collard greens, kale, cavolo nero, chard...

> 150g chopped kale - don't be alarmed at the volume, it reduces hugely once blanched
> ¼ cup extra virgin olive oil
> 2 TBL tamari (intense soya sauce, usually gluten free - please check)
> 1 TBL lemon juice
> 2 grated cloves of fresh garlic

- Put the chopped greens in a large bowl and pour on boiling water. Cover and leave for 5 minutes.
- Pull the greens out with tongs into another bowl, leaving the water behind. Any grit will have sunk to the bottom.
- Let them cool and then pour off any excess water.
- Toss with the oil first, then the tamari, garlic and the lemon juice.

Mexislaw

The use of both red and white cabbage is optional. If only one colour is preferred the slaw will be just as nice.

¼ finely chopped red cabbage (about 1 cup)
¼ finely chopped white cabbage (about 1 cup)
⅓ cup chopped fresh coriander
1 finely diced red chilli
zest and juice of 1 lime
1 TBL olive oil
¼ tsp each of salt and coarsely ground black pepper

- Combine the cabbage, coriander and chilli in a bowl.
- Now toss with the olive oil. Adding the olive oil first coats the cabbage and protects it from the acid of the lime and the leaching of the salt. This matters when using two colours of cabbage as it keeps the white whiter for longer.
- Now the lime zest, juice, salt and pepper.
- Toss and serve.

Coleslaw

A good basic coleslaw is easy to jazz up. Grated apple and onion are frequently added as variations; mustard in the mayo is another.

½ finely chopped white cabbage (about 2 cups)
2 cups of grated carrots
¼ tsp salt and 1 TBL lemon
3 TBL coconut sugar - carrots vary so much in their natural sweetness, check and adjust sugar accordingly
¼ cup of untreated, additive free soya mylk
¾ cup of sunflower oil

- Whizz the soya mylk and add the sunflower oil bit by bit to make the mayonnaise, adding the salt and lemon at the end. There is more about making mayo on p.158.
- Dump the mayo in with the cabbage and the carrots.
- Toss and check for salt and sweetness, adding coconut sugar if required.
- Serve.

Thai salad

This is a recipe
entirely of EL
PIANO's devising
and is Thai insofar
as we have tried
to use the sweet,
hot and crunchy
combinations
that are so
characteristic of
Thai cusine.

Make the Thai red curry paste by whizzing together in a
calibrated jug:

> ¼ cup chopped red chillies
> ¼ cup coconut sugar
> ¼ cup fresh chopped garlic
> ¼ cup sunflower oil or similar light salad oil

- Set aside and enjoy noting how the colour deepens in time.
  You may not need all of this, so jar and refrigerate for use in
  future dishes.

For the salad you will need

> 250g of any noodles. We have used many rice varieties
> 2 peeled and sliced bananas
> 1 head of broccoli cut into florets for steaming,
> reserving the stalk, finely sliced, for frying
> 5 finely chopped spring onions/scallions
> 1 TBL tamari
> 1 tsp lime juice
> ¼ cup salted broad beans, aka habas fritas
> 2 TBL sunflower oil for frying

- Put the bananas and the spring onions/scallions in a large
  salad bowl.
- Set the noodles to cook in accordance with the instructions
  on the packet.
- Steam the florets for about 5 minutes above the noodles in
  order to save time and energy. If the noodles are soak-in-
  boiling-water-only then steam the florets in the ordinary
  way. Ensure that they are irridescent green, not over-cooked,
  pale green. Remove and add to the salad bowl.
- Remove the noodles when cooked and rinse well in cold
  water. Add to the salad bowl.
- Gently fry the broccoli stalks in the oil and 2 TBL red curry
  paste until they are tender but not crisp. Add to the bowl.
- Toss the salad with tamari and lime to taste and garnish
  with the broad beans. Serve.

*We have kept the recipe light for diners who prefer less strong flavours. It's
easy to go up a gear with more tamari and Thai red curry paste.*

Pink salad

Cabbage is available all year round, is inexpensive and hardly used in most kitchens.

You will need:

> *1 cup finely chopped white cabbage*
> *1 cup grated carrot*
> *1 cup grated beetroot*
> *50ml sunflower oil and 50ml orange juice*
> *15ml syrup*
> *10g grated ginger*
> *10ml vinegar*

- *Combine the oil, syrup, grated ginger, orange juice and vinegar.*
- *Pour over the cabbage, carrots and beetroot and serve.*

Potato salad

This potato salad is a classic:

> *1K cubed, boiled, drained and cooled potatoes*
> *½ diced cucumber*
> *½ diced head of celery*
> *50ml pure soya mylk (no additives!)*
> *150ml sunflower oil - no other!*
> *1 TBL lemon juice*
> *2 tsp dried dill or a good bunch of diced fresh dillweed*
> *¼ tsp each of salt and pepper*

- *Whizz the mylk and pour in the sunflower oil steadily. In the final moments it thickens.*
- *Add the lemon juice and salt followed by the dill, reserving some for garnish.*
- *Fold in the potatoes, cucumber and celery.*
- *Top with dill and sprinkled black pepper.*

Variations are mustard in the mayo. For those with an aversion to soya, a vinaigrette is a nice alternative: 3 measures of oil to one of vinegar and then salt, pepper to taste.

Tabuleh

The millet we use in EL PIANO is pearl millet, one of the many versions of this grass that is available from over 500 varieties grown worldwide.

Despite it's wide use it is not a 'cash crop' and therefore tends not to be grown, harvested, dried or stored to a common standard.

The result is that the quality and characteristics of the grain vary from bag to bag.

A more costly, but exceedingly more nutritional alternative is quinoa which is now grown in the UK. The supplier we use is listed on page 221.

The cooking method for quinoa is more predictable. First rinse to wash off any external bitterness. Then boil 1 measure of the grain with 1-2 measures of water (subject to preference). The grains will uncurl and are soft, in about 15 minutes.

It would be nice to be able to tell cooks exactly how to arrive at the light fluffy millet. Sadly every bag that comes into EL PIANO is marginally different from the last...

You will need:

> 200g of millet
> 250ml water with extra water as required
> 200g chopped fresh tomatoes
> 200g fresh chopped cucumber
> 2 cups finely chopped fresh parsley, flat or curly
> 1 TBL extra virgin olive oil
> ¼ tsp salt and 1 TBL lemon juice

- Boil the water. Add the millet and stir well.
- Cover and reduce the heat so that the water simmers. You will need to check it every 5 minutes or so to ensure the grain has not stuck to the bottom of the pan. If the grain is sticking too much and there appears to be little available water, add more.
- When the grains are fluffy, the millet is ready to rinse.
- Rinse and re-rinse until the rinse water is almost clear.
- Drain and combine with the tomatoes, cucumber and parsley.
- Complete the dish by tossing with the olive oil, lemon and salt.

A variation that has been popular in EL PIANO is Moroccan Grain. Leave out the dressing, the tomatoes, cucumber and parsley and add quantities to your preference of:

> raisins
> dates
> sliced dried apricots (ideally non-sulphured - the brown and not the orange!)
> orange zest, cinnamon, ground cumin, green cardamoms
> salt to taste

Over time the fruits will absorb any moisture in the grain and the result is drier with the millet grains being more separated.

Ensalada marco

The origin of the name Marco comes from an Italian, who did amazing things with courgettes, white wine and garlic on the grill. While this is a salad, ungrilled and without white wine, nonethless the association of courgettes and garlic with the name continues.

Simple flavours that emphasise freshness.

You will need

> *50g of quinoa*
> *100ml water and any extra as needed*
> *1 grated courgette*
> *20 ml extra virgin olive oil*
> *1 clove grated garlic*
> *¼ tsp salt and 1 TBL lemon juice (optional)*

- *Fry the garlic in the olive oil until slightly browned.*
- *Remove from the heat and add salt and any lemon juice - we don't add either in EL PIANO. Set aside.*
- *Rinse the quinoa in cold water - this prevents bitterness.*
- *Boil the water and add the quinoa. Keep watch over it and add more water as necessary - it should not boil dry. The grains should uncurl after 15-20 minutes.*
- *Remove from the heat, drain through a seive and cool under running water and leave to drain thoroughly.*
- *Add the grated courgettes and toss with the olive oil.*
- *Serve.*

Mixed leaves

You will need:

> *4 handfuls of any green leaves of your choice, including fresh herbs*
> *150ml sunflower or light salad oil - not olive oil!*
> *½ cup red berries or any mix of red berries*

- *Wash the leaves and drain off as much water as possible.*
- *Whizz together the oil and the fruit.*
- *Toss both together and serve.*

We try and make our salads really simple in EL PIANO on the grounds that the fresher they are, the better. Wherever possible we leave the salt out.

Fresh tomato salsa

There is something so satisfying about such fresh, simple dishes.

Big E (as opposed to Little E), has been cooking in EL PIANO since 2010 and has her own take on the Mexican classic.

Always better if made fresh on the day, but then left an hour at room temperature for the flavours to combine.

All you will need is:

> 1K chopped fresh tomatoes - mixed colours gives a great visual effect
> 1 finely diced red onion
> ⅓ cup chopped fresh coriander
> 1½ tsp salt

- Combine, leave to rest and serve.

Big E salsa

This is exactly as the fresh tomato salsa but with some additions:

> 2 chopped kiwi fruit
> 1-2 chopped or minced fresh red chillies
> Juice and zest of 1 lime

Fresh green salsa

The green of this salsa intensifies as it is left to stand. It's a fantastic addition to any Mediterranean or Latin American dish, either as a fresh topping or as a base to pizza or tostadas.

All you will need is:

> 2 cored and de-seeded green peppers
> 2 coarsely chopped white onions

- Combine in a bowl and whizz.

Salsas that are not used on the day they are made, or on the day after, can be readily used as a base for soup. A drop of olive oil in the pan, then fry the salsa before adding other ingredients of your choice. Pre-cooked black beans are our favourite addition.

5
Mains

Banana curry

When our friend Miranda travelled to the West Indies in the late 1970s she returned to London with stories of a banana curry, served in the streets on banana leaves.

The idea captured us and decades later, when we were asked to provide free food for a benefit for orangutans, we pondered, 'What might an orangutan like to eat if invited to their benefit?'

The idea of a banana curry surfaced from Miranda's tales of her travels so many years before...

An EL PIANO original, the story behind the recipe as told by Magdalena is at the side. We have made this dish for high days and holidays in EL PIANO and for many years it was the staple fayre we offered during the Festival of Angels - not be confused with the novel of the same name, written as a celebration of that event. There is one big hint to share - peeling bananas takes a great deal longer than one might think, especially when peeling many kilos.

3 TBL minced fresh ginger
3 TBL minced fresh garlic
1 diced white onion
8 peeled and sliced bananas
2 TBL Madras curry powder
100g creamed coconut, chopped up
50g chopped fresh coriander
50ml sunflower oil
2 tsp salt (maybe more or less depending on the size of the bananas
400ml water

- Sauté the ginger, garlic and onion in the oil until translucent.
- Add the Madras curry powder and the bananas and fry until the bananas are coated in the oil and spice.
- Add the water and then the creamed coconut.
- Bring to the boil. Coconut is a natural thickener so add any water to bring the curry to the consistency you prefer.
- Remove from the heat and stir in the coriander and the salt.
- Serve.

Frito seco

Turmeric is purported to have many curative properties and is increasingly available as a root.

Just like rubbing up against the stamens of lilies, turmeric is the devil to remove from clothing or plastic containers. Many times we are obliged to discard our plastic jugs in EL PIANO due to the staining. So avoid using anything other than ceramic or metal.

Or so we write here... However, Bob managed to stain a cermaic sink that was slightly crazed when staying at some friends' house. He caught the error quickly and loads of elbow grease later managed to save the day.

For anyone who says they don't like curry, this is a fantastic place to start to try and encourage their enthusiasm. Aromatic and easy to digest it is so simple it barely warrants a page of its own. Yet it is a staple in our family kitchen.

Pre-heat the oven to medium hot. Oil two oven trays.

> 2K cubed potatoes
> 3 TBL fennel seeds
> 2 TBL turmeric
> 300ml water
> 50g grated ginger
> 2 TBL salt (1 TBL per tray)
> 50ml sunflower oil or similar (not olive oil!) for coating the potatoes

- Mix the water, ginger and turmeric in a jug.
- Mix the cubed potatoes, fennel seeds, oil and salt in a large bowl until the potatoes are fully coated.
- Divide the potato mix between the two oven trays and put them to roast them in the oven.
- When the potatoes are almost cooked through, but not quite crispy golden, 20-30 minutes, depending on the size of the cubes, remove the trays from the oven.
- Divide the contents of the jug between the two trays, moving the potatoes around on the trays so that they are coated by the fluid.
- Return the trays to the oven for another 10 minutes or so, until the fluid has baked off and the potatoes are crispy.
- Serve.

Sweet & sour tofu

The sweet and sour sauce is easy to adapt and use for other dishes.

Despite the title, for those who dislike tofu, this is as good a dish without the bean curd.

Prepare the tofu:

>*400g tofu cut into squares*
>*100g rice flour*
>*200ml water*
>*1 TBL black pepper*
>*1 tsp salt*
>*Sunflower oil or light salad oil for frying (not olive oil!)*

- Make a batter of the water, flour, salt and pepper.
- Dip the tofu in the batter and then deep fry until crispy.
- Drain and set aside.

Prepare the sweet and sour:

>*1 chopped red onion*
>*1 each red and yellow peppers, chopped*
>*8 quartered button mushrooms*
>*¼ fresh pineapple, chopped*
>*1 bunch chopped spring onions/scallions*
>*100g fresh bean sprouts*
>*20g grated fresh ginger*
>*4 TBL tamari*
>*2 TBL coconut sugar*
>*2 TBL tomato paste*
>*2 TBL cornflour or cornstarch*
>*50ml sunflower oil*

- Combine the tamari, tomato paste, sugar and cornflour with 300ml water for the sauce. Mix and set aside.
- Fry the red onion, mushrooms and peppers in the oil for about 5 minutes, so that the veg are cooked but still crunchy.
- Add the sauce mix and stir until thickened, about 5-10 minutes, and, since we can never know how much fluid any veg will contain, add water if required.
- Remove from the heat.
- Finally fold in the pineapple, bean sprouts, spring onions/ scallions.
- Serve, placing the tofu on the top.

Migas

The word 'migas' is Spanish for 'crumbs' and is a dish that can be found throughout the Hispanic world.

Originally the 'crumbs' were stale bread, crumbed up and then drenched in olive oil, or even pig fat, and mixed with seasonal vegetables.

Nowadays many people make their migas by going out and buying bread crumbs from the supermarket which somehow takes away from it's appeal.

Ultimately migas is a peasant dish: few inexpensive ingredients that make use of what is local and/or can be recycled. Bread and butter pudding being a British example of such a dish.

This is a weird one for those who have not lived in Spain. But it reminds us of our many years there and, although this is in the mains section, and is often served as a meal in itself, it is improved when served with salad.

Prepare the crumbs:

> 250g polenta
> 50ml extra virgin olive oil
> 450ml water

- Cook the polenta slowly in the oil and water over a low heat.
- When the polenta has fully absorbed the fluid remove from the heat and cover.
- Set aside.
- When cool to the touch, crumb it up and leave it in a large bowl.

Prepare the vegetables:

> 1 chopped red onion
> 2 chopped green peppers
> 1 bunch chopped spring onions/scallions
> 6 cloves coarsely chopped fresh garlic
> 6 thinly sliced sun-dried tomatoes - these must be soft and easy to eat
> 50ml extra virgin olive oil
> 1 tsp salt

- Fry everything except the sun-dried tomatoes and the salt in the olive oil until the veg is cooked yet still crunchy.
- Remove from the heat and combine with the crumbs.
- Add the sun-dried tomatoes and salt.

Kofta with turmeric sauce

The sauce is Sri Lankan in origin, taught to us by Kundia who used it mostly as a sauce for boiled eggs.

It makes use of the chalky quality of turmeric and is immensely cleansing on the palate and the gut.

Kofta is a common dish from the Middle East eastwards and varies in flavour from the spicy to the benign. This is a fiery version that can be damped down by reducing the chillies.

First the turmeric sauce:

> 8 diced spring onions/scallions
> 2 sliced red chillies
> 2 TBL sunflower oil
> 2 TBL turmeric
> 100g creamed coconut steeped in 500ml hot water
> 1 tsp salt

- *Sauté the chillies and half of the spring onions/scallions, reserving the other half for garnish.*
- *Add the turmeric for just a moment so as not to change the colour from yellow to brown by scorching it.*
- *Now add the creamed coconut and water. Bring to the boil.*
- *Remove from the heat, add the salt and set aside.*

The kofta:

> 1 finely diced white onion
> 1 cup plain textured soya protein (TVP)
> 1 TBL curry powder
> 1 tsp salt
> 100ml sunflower oil for the shallow frying
> Sunflower oil or similar light salad oil for deep or shallow frying
> 1-2 TBL chickpea flour aka gram, besan or garbanzo bean flour

- *Fry the onion and the spices in the 100ml of oil.*
- *Add the TVP. Stir so that it absorbs the oil yet does not burn.*
- *Add 500ml of water, cover and cook on a low heat, checking periodically to ensure it has not simmered dry.*
- *When the water is absorbed, and the TVP is uniformly soft, about 20-30 minutes, remove from the heat.*
- *Now add the flour and enough water so the mix binds yet is still sticky.*
- *With wet hands, form into balls and fry, ensuring all sides are brown.*
- *Remove. Serve topped with the turmeric sauce and garnish.*

Shepherd's pie

Elaina has cooked in EL PIANO since 2010 and is a fantastic traditional, English, domestic cook. She has brought up 3 children and is now bringing up 4 more.

She serves up meals every day to a minimum of 6 people and shepherd's pie is a staple.

This is her version for EL PIANO and contains no soya - textured vegetable protein (TVP).

First the potato topping:

> 8 large potatoes each cut into 6
> 100ml extra virgin olive oil
> 1 tsp salt and ½ tsp black pepper

- Boil the potates until they are soft and breaking up.
- Drain and then mash the potatoes with the olive oil adding the salt and pepper.

Now the filling:

> 20 button mushrooms
> 2 carrots cut into coins
> 2 chopped white onions
> 200g frozen peas
> 200g drained tinned beans (optional)
> 200ml extra virgin olive oil
> 2 TBL buckwheat flour
> 4 TBL yeast extract

- Sauté all the veg, except the peas, in the olive oil for 15-20 minutes.
- Remove from the heat and stir in the buckwheat flour.
- Add 500ml water and the yeast extract and return to the heat, stirring constantly until the mix thickens.
- Stir in the frozen peas and any beans.
- Divide the mix between 4 oven proof dishes or place it all into one larger dish.
- Wet your hands, as sticky things do not stick to wet hands, and take the mash potato mix in handfuls and flatten it between your palms laying it across the filling until the filling is fully covered.
- Score the potato covering with a fork to create ridges.
- Baste with olive oil and sprinkle with black pepper.
- Bake in a medium oven, 20-40 minutes until the potato topping is brown and crusty.
- Serve.

Paella with chorizo

This was on the menu throughout the summer of 2016. It was a rare UK summer with many fine days. More often than not we cooked the paella outside over the open burner.

The hiziki seaweed gave it the fishy taste and smell that many omnivores crave and the chorizo was beyond delicious.

Reconstitute the hiziki by steeping it in boiling water for 15 minutes. Then drain it and add it to the cooked paella. If cooked with the rice it turns it all a purple-green!

The chorizo are a lot of work, but like the bangers on p.132, once you are set up and making them, you may as well make a lot.

We tend not freeze anything in EL PIANO but these are one of the few things we make where freezing does not seem to diminish their taste or texture.

First the chorizo:

> 500g any type of finely chopped mushroom
> 500g chopped aubergine
> 20 cloves of sliced garlic
> 3 TBL smoked paprika and 1½ TBL salt
> 330-400g rice flour
> 100ml extra virgin olive oil
> Cling film or 'saran' wrap

- Fry veg, garlic, paprika and salt in the olive oil for 15-20 minutes.
- Remove from the heat. Whizz, leaving some texture. Cool.
- Prepare a steam bath. We use a wire rack over boiling water.
- Now add the flour bit by bit, stirring it through the mix.
- Put a roll of cling film or 'saran' wrap behind a flat chopping board so that it's easy to roll out directly onto the board.
- Lay a long sausage of mix along the plastic from left to right. Leave the edge of the film nearest to you free.
- Pull on the film, wrap it over the sausage. Roll it on the board to enclose it in the film and seal the ends by pressing them down.
- Run a knife across the film at the back on the board to separate the film from the roll. There is a picture guide on p.218.
- Place the chorizo on the rack over the boiling water and turn them regularly. When they become firm they are ready.
- To use immediately, or later, remove the film and pan fry.

Now the paella:

> 3 chopped red peppers and 1 chopped red onion
> 2 tsp turmeric
> 250g frozen peas
> 50g reconstituted dried hiziki - see the side bar
> 10 cloves sliced, but chunky, fresh garlic
> 100ml extra virgin olive oil
> 250g paella rice
> 250ml white wine and 750ml water.

- Sauté the peppers, garlic and onions in the olive oil.
- Add the tumeric and then the rice, followed by all the fluid.
- Cook until the rice is soft, adding more water as required.
- Remove from the heat and fold in the hiziki and the peas.
- Crown with the cooked chorizo and serve.

Chilli sin carne

This dish requires no accompaniments beyond a bowl and a spoon. It is great when served over a bed of pam rice, p.118 or with corn bread, p.42.

This is one of few recipes in this book where we use textured vegetable protein (TVP). It's an easy recipe to scale up to make moutains of chilli and is a useful easy meal to provide extra ballast at events like weddings and family parties.

You will need:

> *1 x 400g tin of red kidney beans, drained*
> *3-4 whole fresh red chillies*
> *1 chopped large white onion*
> *2L whizzed tomatoes*
> *4 cups textured vegetable protein (TVP)*
> *250ml extra virgin olive oil*
> *2 TBL salt.*

- *Sauté the chillies and the onion in the olive oil.*
- *Add the TVP and stir it into the oil taking care not to scorch it. If you do, throw it all away and start over... Burned soy products generally are disgusting.*
- *Add the tomatoes.*
- *Cover and let it cook slowly for 30-40 minutes taking care that it doesn't catch on the bottom of the pan.*
- *When the TVP is fully cooked and soft, remove from the heat and add the salt and tip in the kidney beans.*
- *Serve.*

Fresh fruit curry

The aim of preparing naked orange segments is to leave behind the peel, the pith and the membrane around the orange segments so that all is left are the tiny little orange sacs full of juice. Use a sharp knife. Slice the top and the bottom off an orange. Rest it on a board. Slice the peel off from the top to the bottom, curving the knife inward to ensure that all the pith is removed with the peel.

Pick up the orange. It is easy to see how the peeling has exposed the collection of naked little sacs of orange juice that form each segment. Cut into the centre of the fruit cutting between the sacs and the segment membrane. Release the whole segment which is now free of both peel and membrane. These are the naked orange segments. The membrane left behind can then be squeezed in your hand to release all the residual juice.

Feel free to make this with a host of fruit, it's colourful and intriguing and generally people like it, but our favourite is made with less, not more...

Prepare the sambal oelek, a fearsome chilli paste:

> 100g coconut sugar
> 100g minced red chillies
> 100g minced garlic
> 100ml of lime juice

- Whizz together and set aside.

That which is not used can be jarred and refrigerated, remembering, once stored, to only ever use it when cooking and never raw on toast or in salad dressings. The rational for this is discussed on p.142.

For the curry you will need:

> 2 sliced, large plantain
> 8 oranges in naked segments and the residual juice
> - see the side bar for the instructions for this
> 100g dessicated coconut - more or less to taste
> 2 sliced white onion (optional)
> the juice of 1 lime
> 1 tsp salt
> sunflower oil for frying

- Dot some sunflower oil in a frying pan and heat to hot-hot.
- Add 2 TBL of the sambal oelek and fry, but do not burn.
- Throw in the plantain and any onion, and brown well.
- Add the dessicated coconut and stir constantly so it browns evenly.
- Reduce the heat and add the orange segments followed by the residual orange juice and cook gently.
- When the coconut has absorbed the orange juice remove from the heat.
- Squeeze the lime juice over it all and serve.

Clever quiches

The bean crust quiche was the result of a mistake in EL PIANO in Granada... Exciting new knowledge can result from some kitchen disasters.

Spinach quiche, first make the pastry case

> 100g tofu
> 50g buckwheat flour plus extra for rolling out

- Crumb together the tofu and the buckwheat flour in a bowl.
- Sprinkle in a few drops of water until the dough comes away from the bowl cleanly.
- Roll out the pastry on a floured surface and use to line a 1500ml mould.
- Bake 10 minutes in a medium oven.

Now the spinach filling:

> 1 bunch washed raw spinach
> 200g tofu
> 400ml soya mylk
> 1 chopped diced onion
> 3 TBL corn flour or corn starch
> 2 tsp salt and 1 tsp nutmeg plus a bit for garnish

- Whizz all of the ingredients in a jug.
- Pour over the baked tofu pastry base.
- Sprinkle a bit more nutmeg over the top and bake in a medium oven until firm, about 30-40 minutes.

For bean crust quiche:

> 2 x 400g tinned cannelloni beans
> 6 TBL corn flour/cornstarch
> 2 TBL oregano or mixed herbs
> 1K chopped vegetables such as mushrooms, peppers, courgettes and 1 chopped large white onion
> 3 TBL extra virgin olive oil, plus some to oil the dish
> 1 tsp salt

- Sauté the vegetables and the onion in the olive oil.
- Whizz the beans, corn flour/cornstarch and herbs together.
- Pour the whizzed beans onto an oven roasting tray.
- Place the fried vegetable mix evenly across the bean mix.
- Bake in a medium oven for 30-40 minutes.
- The bean mix will rise around the edges and harden like a crust.

Pumpkin curry

You can just as easily use butternut squash. This recipe is a largely dry and slightly sweet curry due to the onions and squash.

1K of chopped squash - no need to peel it unless the outer skin is really tough
2 finely diced white onion
2 TBL black mustard seeds
50g grated, unpeeled, fresh ginger
100g grated fresh garlic
2 TBL Madras curry powder
1 whole red chilli
1 TBL salt
50ml sunflower oil or similar (not olive oil!)

- Sauté everything in the oil for about 3 minutes.
- Reduce the heat and cover.
- Cook for 15-20 minutes under cover until the squash is soft.
- Remove from the heat and serve.

This method can be used for mixed vegetable curry just as well, provided the vegetables will cook more or less at the same rate. It's no good for example pairing mushrooms and carrots, or potatoes with bean sprouts. Choose an ensemble of veg that have roughly the same cooking times.

The burger

Elsewhere in this book we have endeavoured to keep all the recipes needed for any dish on one page. Thus things are repeated to maximise the cook's efficiency. This is the only recipe in the book which will force you to endlessly flip back and forth, page to page.

Bob's big burger is well known in EL PIANO as a massive taste treat and this page tells you where to go in the book to find out how to make it. You will need the bread bun, the burger, the condiments and the salads.

THE BREAD BUN
Bread - p.38

THE BURGER
Any 3 fritter mixes combined. Bob's personal favourites are:
Corn Fritter mix p.46
Falafel Mix - p.58
Mushroom and garlic mix - p.48

THE CONDIMENTS
Hummus - p.16
Mayo - p.158
Red Lead - p.156
Dill pickle - p.166
Peruvian green sauce - p.144 (Bob's personal favourite - thank you Miriam!)

SIDE SALADS
Any will do, but Bob's personal favourites are:
Guacamole - p.28
Smoked sauerkraut - p.62
Any of the salsas - p.82

Off you go.... ha ha ha.

Send us an email if you ever make this...
elpiano21yearsfree@gmail.com

Corn balls in molé

Molé sauce, a deep and rich savoury chocolate sauce can have up to 40 ingredients. There isn't a family in Mexico who doesn't have the definitive and best family recipe for molé sauce.

Our recipe is basic yet fiesty, and is a great platform upon which to make any personal alterations.

An acquired taste, but for those who love it, it's stellar. Beware the chocolate chips, although they enhance the dish, the make the oil filthy.

First the molé sauce:

> *2 peeled bananas broken into 3 or 4 pieces*
> *1 tsp of cayenne pepper or ground dried chillies*
> *1 tsp coriander seeds*
> *3 TBL cocoa powder*
> *1 tsp cinnamon*
> *1 tsp salt*
> *juice of 2 limes*
> *50-75ml water*

- Put all of the ingredients in a jug and whizz, adding the water as needed for a pouring consistency like molton chocolate.
- Adjust seasoning and set aside

Now the corn balls:

> *1 400g tinned sweet corn, drained and whizzed*
> *2-4 diced fresh red chillies*
> *1 bunch of chopped, fresh coriander*
> *1 diced white onion (optional)*
> *1 TBL salt*
> *2 TBL sugar-free chocolate chips (optional)*
> *100g rice flour plus a bit extra if needed*
> *Sunflower oil or similar (not olive oil!) for frying*

- Put everything except the flour and the oil in a bowl.
- Add the flour, just enough so the balls will hold together in the fryer. If they don't hold together, add a touch more flour.
- Form into balls and fry in hot sunflower oil removing when evenly golden.
- Serve topped with the molé sauce and garnish.

Cous cous

For many years we made this dish with millet and nearly lost our minds as millet is such a difficult grain to use predictably.

We resisted buying quinoa as, until recently, quinoa was harvested largely in South America. This had two distadvantages for us in terms of our buying policies. Firstly it was hardly local. Secondly far too many people local to quinoa were prevented from buying it for their own diets due to its costs.

Happily in 2015 we found that quinoa was being farmed organically in the UK. More information about our suppliers is available on p.221

It makes no difference it there is more quinoa and fewer vegetables or vice versa. Moreover it is easy to bulk up the recipe to serve more people. This is a really fast dish to make, and, once assembled, cooks itself whilst freeing you to do other things. As it has no oil it is remarkably fresh and light for a cooked dish.

Toss together:

    300g quinoa
    1 carrot sliced in coins
    4 halved small potatoes
    1 coarsley chopped red onion
    200g (½ tin/can) chick peas
    6 chopped dates
    6 sliced dried brown (unsulphered) apricots
    1 courgettes sliced in coins
    1 parsnips sliced in coins
    ½ large chopped sweet potato
    4 green cardamoms
    1 broken sticks of cinnamon
    zest of 1 oranges
    1 TBL salt

- Place the lot in a steamer for 35-45 minutes until the quinoa has uncurled.
- Adjust seasoning and serve.

Chickpea & potato curry

Another great classic from Sakina Begum from East West Kitchen. She not only shared this business recipe with us years ago, she also often served this at home.

By using unsoaked chick peas of course the whole dish takes longer to cook. However the benefit is that the chickpeas absorb the flavours of the curry, rather than the water they are soaked in, or the brine of the tinned variety.

Do not be tempted to take short cuts with this dish.

It's the broth of this curry that makes it exceptional and so satisfying. It is best cooked in a slow cooker. If you have one that allows you to fry before setting it to slow cook, do that. The recipe is written for those who need to transfer from the frying process to a slow cooker. A pressure cooker for this dish is not recommended.

100g uncooked and unsoaked chickpeas
1 TBL grated ginger
500ml of tinned chopped tomatoes, top up to 1L with chopped fresh ones
1 TBL of fresh grated garlic
½ large diced white onion
2 medium potatoes, each cut equally into pieces that are roughly 2.5cm or 1 inch cubes, about 16 per potato
100 ml sunflower oil
1 TBL Madras curry powder
1 TBL dried fenugreek leaves, aka methi
1 TBL salt.

- Wash the chickpeas checking for, and discarding stones and dirt. (After many years of doing this we have begun to think that there is a factory somewhere devoted to making stones shaped and coloured like chickpeas just for introducing into the harvest. So have your wits about you.)
- In a large deep pan with a lid, sauté the garlic, onion and ginger in the oil.
- Add and fry the Madras curry powder, then the potatoes, and fry them briefly.
- Reduce the heat, add the tomatoes and the chickpeas.
- Bring to the boil.
- Either transfer to a covered slow cooker and leave overnight or cover and leave on the lowest heat 8-10 hours on the stove. If cooking on the stove, check hourly, adding water if needed.
- As the potatoes take less time to cook than the chickpeas, they will begin to break up which thickens the broth.
- When the chick peas are soft remove from the heat.
- Only now add the salt.
- Rub the fenugreek between your hands and sprinkle over the curry before serving.

Breaded pie

Cannelloni beans and butter beans are quite distinct from each other in terms of flavour and texture. What they share is their colour which is why we use them in this recipe - the result being a white, creamy filling reminiscent of chicken pie - tofu squares is also an option.

A comfort dish for the cold weather that requires no pastry making! Those of you who have engaged in making gluten-free pastry will know what a challenge that can be. In our earlier book, THE FINAL TOUCH we offer a blow-by-blow recipe with stage by stage photographs tackling gluten-free pastry for pasties. But here, there is no such requirement.

For the topping you will need:

>*200g of bread crumbs - we use day old bread that we make here, but any old bread will do*
>*50ml extra virgin olive oil*
>*dried herbs of your choice to taste*
>*2 tsp nutritional yeast (optional)*
>*1 tsp salt*

- Crumb up the dry bread by hand or in the blender.
- Add the olive oil, herbs and salt.
- Set aside.

For the filling you will need:

>*12 halved button mushrooms, quartered if large*
>*2 sliced carrots*
>*400g frozen peas*
>*400g cooked cannelloni or butter beans*
>*2 TBL extra virgin olive oil*
>*3 TBL rice flour*
>*750ml plant mylk, soya is preferred as it is creamy*
>*1 tsp ground nutmeg*
>*2 tsp salt*

- Sauté the mushrooms and the carrots in the olive oil.
- Add the flour, then the mylk and bring to the boil, stirring constantly to avoid lumps as it thickens.
- Remove from the heat, stir in the nutmeg and add the frozen peas and the beans.
- Add the salt.
- Divide the mix between 4 cazuelas/individual oven proof dishes and top equally with the bread crumbs and any nutritional yeast.
- Bake in a medium oven for 20 minutes or until the bread crumbs are toasted.
- Serve.

Pam rice

Here it is...how to cook rice flawlessly...

Decide the volume of rice you are going to cook and boil twice that volume of water.

Tip the rice into the boiling water. Stir it maybe three times to make sure it will not stick. Lower the heat, cover and leave 20 minutes.

Do not look at it. Do not chat to it. Just leave it with the lid on on a low heat.

That's it. Perfect every time.

We have to thank THE OLD COOP in Todmorden West Yorkshire for this rice. When we opened EL PIANO in Granada Pam Warhurst came to visit and, typically, got her sleeves rolled up and got stuck to help us out. The result is definitely a nod toward the Middle East and Persia, and it's a meal in itself.

4 chopped large aubergines
At least 20 cloves of garlic, sliced coarsely
2 TBL olive oil
400g brown basmati rice, pre-soaked
1L water
80g chopped parsley
200ml of tamari
40ml lemon juice

- Sauté the aubergines and garlic in the olive oil for about 5 minutes. The aubergines will suck up all the oil and the garlic will brown.
- Add the rice and then the water.
- Cover and cook on a low heat until all the water is absorbed, about 20 minutes.
- Remove from the heat.
- Season with the tamari and lemon.
- Finally fold in the fresh parsley.
- Serve.

This is also perfect as a filling for stuffed pumpkin. Follow the recipe above but don't add the water!

Mix it all together and spoon into a pumpkin that has had the seeds removed.

Pop the lid of the pumkin on top and bake in the oven. Essentially all the fluid of the pumpkin becomes the 'water' for the rice.

The pumpkin is ready when the sides are soft.

Pan fried tofu

For people who eat a lot of tofu there is merit in making your own at home. You need a thermometer and nigari, a mineral salt from Japan, as the coagulant.

Using unadulterated soya mylk, heat it to boiling and maintain it at a boil for about 2-3 minutes. The idea is to kill off any contaminants.

Take care not let it burn. If it does, throw it away and start over. Burnt soya mylk is simply inedible.

Remove from the heat and let it cool to 70°- 80°. Add 10g of nigari for every 1L of mylk. Stir once, twice, thrice. Not a stroke more. Leave it at least 20 minutes, then strain through cheese cloth in a colander and weight it with a plate and some other things, allowing it to drip, ideally overnight.

Taa Daa! Tofu.

So many people who come to our COOKSCHOOL struggle to know what to do with tofu. The seasoned vegans are well versed, but people new to reducing meat and fish in their diet have heard that tofu is a key ingredient and then discover that to eat it is not unlike chewing the inside of one's cheek. This recipe is great for a fancy meal but it is totally amazing in sandwiches.

Classic:

> 400g block of tofu cut into slices about 1/2 inch or 1cm thick - Bob loves it thin.
> 1 bunch of diced spring onions/scallions
> 30g grated, unpeeled fresh ginger
> tamari to taste
> sunflower oil or similar light oil (not olive oil!)

- Oil a pan or griddle to hot-hot.
- Throw on a few bits of the chopped spring onions/scallions and some of the grated ginger.
- Follow this quickly with the slabs of tofu. Sear the tofu on both sides.
- Now a dash of tamari to taste, turning the steak as required. For those who prefer a savoury, crispy result this is the moment to leave it longer to crisp up.
- Remove and serve with some spring onion/scallion garnish.

With green pepper sauce:

> 400g block of tofu cut into slices about 1/2 inch or 1cm thick
> 3 TBL green hydrated peppercorns from a jar
> 2 TBL buckwheat flour
> 1 glass white wine, 30ml brandy and 200ml soya mylk
> Extra virgin olive oil and black pepper to taste

- Prepare the sauce by draining the peppercorns. Sauté them in 2 TBL of the olive oil.
- Remove from the heat and stir in 3 TBL buckwheat flour.
- Add the fluid, stir until thickened, adjust seasoning. Whizz.
- Oil a frying pan with olive oil and heat to hot-hot.
- Sear the steaks on both sides to the desired crispiness.
- Remove from the heat and serve with the green pepper sauce.

Thai duo

In a way this is a fusion dish... flavours of Thailand but topped with Japanese tofu.

The key to the success of this dish is the colourful variety of the vegetables and ensuring that the vegetables are not over-cooked. Feel free to change the vegetables for any you may prefer.

First make the sweet chilli sauce for the final drizzle:

> 50g minced fresh red chillies
> 75ml syrup
> 1 cup of coconut sugar
> 100g fresh garlic
> 75ml sunflower oil
> ½ tsp salt and ½ a lemon

- Cook everything except the lemon in a pan for 10 minutes.
- Add the half lemon, the entire half, and whizz.

Now the Thai-style vegetable broth:

> 1 red onion
> 2 sliced carrots
> 1 sliced red pepper
> 1 head of broccoli cut into florets
> 1 stalk of lemongrass, cut lengthways from above the root so it stays together and also releases the flavour
> 3 dried or fresh lime leaves
> 45g grated sliced fresh ginger
> 100g creamed coconut
> 100ml tamari
> 1 TBL sunflower oil

- Sauté the ginger, lemongrass and all of the vegetables, except the broccoli, for about 3 minutes in the oil.
- Add 700ml water, the coconut and lime leaves.
- When the vegetables are just cooked through, remove from the heat. Add the broccoli florets and tamari. Cover the pan.

While the broccoli softens, prepare the tofu :

> 400g sliced, firm tofu
> rice flour for dusting
> Sunflower oil for frying

- Heat the oil in a pan or in the deep fat fryer.
- Dust the tofu with the rice flour and then fry until golden.

Hook out the lemongrass from the broth. Assemble the dish: first the broth, then the tofu then the sweet chilli sauce. Serve.

In EL PIANO we serve this on a bed of rice.

Mani mani

Toasted broad beans, or habas fritas are a staple snack food, in Spain.

They are a nutty addition to any meal. For those who are allergic to nuts these are a satisfactory alternative, either whole, or ground.

Take care to read the ingredients labels as many snacks are packaged using machines where nuts are also processed.

This is a derivation of a Botswanan groundnut stew recipe. It's very simple but surprisingly delicious and has always been a great favourite at EL PIANO any time it is on the menu. It may seem like a lot of peppers, but remember they are hollow!

500g diced mixed coloured peppers
250g toasted broad beans aka habas fritas
1 finely chopped, cleaned, leek - cut the leek lengthways in four, stopping just short of the roots. Now it is easy to wash it under the tap to remove any grit without them all falling apart
500g coarsely chopped tomatoes
1 TBL turmeric
25ml extra virgin olive oil
1 tsp salt - this may vary depending on how salty the habas fritas are

- Sauté the leek, peppers and tumeric in the olive oil for about 3-5 minutes.
- When the veg are softened but not browned, add the tomato, salt and broad beans.
- Stew over gentle heat until the tomatoes have disintegrated, about 20 minutes.
- Whizz it to your desired texture.
- Add the salt and serve..

In EL PIANO we serve mani mani on a bed of wholegrain rice. Although this recipe salutes a peasant dish from one of the poorest areas of the world, like most peasant fare it's deeply satisfying.

Mini moussaka

By baking the vegetables first and then stuffing the mushrooms the risk of over-cooking the mushrooms is lost. And there is also no danger of the potatoes not cooking through.

The bechamel sauce is based on the French classic and is extremely versatile.

It works well for macaroni or cauliflower cheese as well as being a good base for Hollandaise sauce.

Flours can differ. Using chickpea flour will give a more yellow appearance, buckwheat flour tends toward the grey and maize is both yellow and grainy in texture. Cocoa powder, also a bean 'flour' will take the sauce into custards and sweet sauces. The basic chemistry is in the recipe and it's open to the cook to adapt it.

This recipe is best approached on a per head basis and calls for portobello or field mushrooms as they are generally huge and one mini moussaka will usually serve for one diner! They are also great as a starter.

You will need:

> 4 portobello mushrooms
> 2 sliced white potatoes
> 1 large aubergine sliced into 12 coins
> 24 cherry tomatoes
> 2 tsp oregano
> splash of olive oil and 1 tsp salt

- Wash and set the mushrooms aside.
- Toss all the prepared vegetables in the olive oil and salt and bake in a medium oven until soft, 15-20 minutes.

While these bake, make a batch of 'cheesy' bechamel sauce:
> 1 TBL extra virgin olive oil
> 1½ TBL rice flour
> 250ml rice mylk or other plant mylk
> 1 tsp mustard and 1 tsp salt
> 100ml white wine
> ½ cup nutritional yeast

- Heat the extra virgin olive oil in a pan. Remove from the heat and stir in the rice flour so that the flour is well coated by the oil. Return to the heat and add the mylk and yeast.
- Stir constantly until the sauce thickens.
- Finally stir in the mustard, salt and the wine. Set aside.

Assemble the mini mousaka:

- Place the fresh washed mushrooms upside down on an oiled baking tray.
- Layer the vegetables equally into each mushroom.
- Top each with a good dollop of the bechamel sauce.
- Put the tray in the oven and bake until the mushrooms are cooked - about 15-20 minutes.
- Remove. Garnish with chopped greenery, black pepper or paprika or all three!
- Serve.

El Piano's classic

Dhal simply means lentil in Hindi. For years when we were calling it lentil dhal we were just repeating ourselves! It's often merely a thin gruel to pour over rice, or thicker to eat with wheat chappatti. This combining of grains with legumes is prevalent in most classic dishes the world over. For the UK? Beans on toast of course!

Inspired by Jack Santa Maria, this dish has never been off the EL PIANO menu.

200g split red lentils
20g grated ginger
1 chopped white onion
20 cloves of fresh sliced garlic
4 TBL sunflower oil
1 TBL Madras curry powder
100g creamed coconut
40g chopped, fresh coriander and 2 tsp salt

- Sauté the garlic, onion and ginger in the oil.
- Add and fry the Madras curry powder.
- Now the lentils, and fry them briefly.
- Reduce the heat, add 1 L of water and the coconut.
- Continue cooking on a low heat until the lentils dissolve.
- Remove from the heat, add the salt and the coriander.

Tarka dhal

Sakeena Begum from East West Kitchen shared this recipe with us years ago. It's much lower fat than our classic dhal, and, has no onions, which some customers prefer.

200g brown lentils
20g grated ginger
500ml of fresh or tinned chopped tomatoes
20 cloves of fresh sliced garlic
4 TBL sunflower oil
1 TBL Madras curry powder
1 TBK dried fenugreek leaves aka methi and 2 tsp salt.

- Sauté the garlic and ginger in the oil.
- Add, and fry, the Madras curry powder.
- Now add the lentils, and fry them briefly.
- Reduce the heat, add the tomatoes, and any water needed as the lentils should not cook dry.
- Remove when the lentils are soft. Add the salt.
- Rub the fenugreek between your hands and sprinkle over the top before serving.

Tortilla española

A good trick in the kitchen when dealing with anything sticky is to remember that very little sticks to water...

Tortilla is hugely forgiving. If, when you turn it, it falls on the floor, into the sink, breaks over the counter top, simply gather up all the parts and ram it back into the pan, smashing it all together. You'll be amazed at how easily it retains its shape and how well it serves up.

Tortilla will keep at least a week in the fridge. Easy to carve off slices for snacks and sandwiches, it is the ideal fare for packed lunches and picnics.

During the 'hungry years' around the Spanish Civil War a common substitute for eggs was ground chickpeas. This truly is a spanish recipe... And, like peasant dishes the world over it's simple, inexpensive to make and intensely satisfying.

All you will need are

> 1 K potatoes
> 1 large onion or 2 smaller ones
> 1 cup of chickpea flour (gram/besan/garbanzo bean) flour
> 100ml + a bit more, extra virgin olive oil
> 1½ TBL salt

- Slice the potatoes and onion uniformly. The thinner they are sliced, the faster they will cook.
- Place them in a bowl and salt generously. 1½ TBL salt may seem a lot, but the salt pulls out the moisture from the veg, then settling with the liquid that is later discarded.
- Set aside for at least 30 minutes.
- Heat half of the oil in a good sized, non-stick frying pan.
- Remove the potates and onion from the salty fluid, and place them in the hot oil.
- Turn them once, reducing the heat, and cover so that they steam-fry - about 20 minutes.
- Meanwhile beat the gram flour with 250ml of water. It will look and feel exactly like beaten eggs. No need for more salt!
- Fold the fully cooked potatoes into the flour mix.
- Return the mix to the frying pan, ensuring that there is a good covering of oil in the pan, adding more if required.
- Push the mix, if necessary, to the edges of the pan. Keep the heat at medium.
- As the edges dry, test that the tortilla is loose by agitating the pan. It should move freely. If not, use a spatula to free it.
- Remove the pan from the heat. Wet a plate that is slightly larger than the pan and invert it over the pan.
- Choose a safe surface over which to then turn the plate and pan, keeping plate and pan pressed tightly together.
- Once the tortilla is on the plate, slide it back into the pan to cook the second side.
- When it is firm it is ready to serve.

Bangers

The science is that rice expands, and this fact means that our bangers hold together!

Cut leeks lengthways in four, stopping just short of the roots. Now they are easy to wash under the tap and remove any grit without them all falling apart.

This dish can as easily be served with regular mash. Swede mash complements the flavour and the colour. Additionally, if reheating is needed, it us superior to potato mash.

Its fiddly, and there is a picture guide on page 218. Once you get set up it's easy to rattle off a freezer full. While we rarely freeze anything at EL PIANO, for the home consumer, a freezer full of bangers for use at any time cannot be a bad thing...

500g any type of chopped mushroom
500g chopped aubergine
1K chopped leeks
60g chopped fresh sage
1 TBL salt and 2 TBL black pepper
330-400g rice flour
100ml extra virgin olive oil
Cling film or 'saran' wrap

- *Cook the veg, sage, salt, pepper and olive oil in a covered pan.*
- *When the veg have all sweated out their juices, about 15-20 minutes, remove from the heat and take off the lid.*
- *Stir the mix so that it cools somewhat. Whizz it to your desired texture.*
- *Leave it to cool further while you prepare a steam bath. We use a wire rack over boiling water.*
- *Now add the flour bit by bit, stirring it through the mix.*
- *Put a roll of cling film or 'saran' wrap behind a flat chopping board so that it's easy to roll out directly onto the board.*
- *Lay a long sausage of mix along the plastic from left to right. Leave the edge of the film nearest to you free.*
- *Pull on the film, wrap it over the sausage. Roll it on the board to enclose it in the film and seal the ends by pressing them down.*
- *Run a knife across the film at the back on the board to separate the film from the roll. There is a picture guide on p.218.*
- *Place the bangers on the rack over the boiling water and turn them regularly. When they become firm they are ready.*
- *To use immediately, or later, remove the film and pan fry.*

In EL PIANO we serve these on a bed of swede mash. Boil ½ swede per person. Drain, mash with extra virgin olive oil, salt and pepper to taste.

Keema mathar

We have largely moved away from textured vegetable protein (TVP) in EL PIANO, as already mentioned in some detail on page 146. The few recipes we have included in 21 YEARS FREE are in recognition of times past, and also to allow some cooks who are more familiar with TVP to remain in their comfort zone before branching off into the 'meat' dishes we make where no soya is used.

As cooks who have long worked in the food industry we have concerns about the overuse of any ingredient.

Keema mathar is 'mince with peas' in Hindi and the mince referred to is generally minced lamb or goat. A further variation of this dish is the kofta on p.94 where the 'meat' mix is highly spiced with chillies and the piquancy then calmed down by the turmeric sauce.

You will need:

>   1 finely diced white onion
>   1 cup plain TVP
>   100g frozen peas
>   1½ tsp cumin
>   4 tsp Madras curry powder
>   1½ - 2 tsp salt
>   100ml sunflower oil or similar light salad oil

- Fry the onion and the spices in the oil.
- Add the TVP and stir so that it absorbs the oil yet does not burn.
- Add 500ml of water, cover and cook on a low heat, checking periodically to ensure it has not simmered dry.
- When the water is absorbed, and the TVP is uniformly soft, about 20-30 minutes, remove from the heat.
- Add the salt. Stir through the frozen peas, cover and let it stand 5 minutes. Serve.

Burned TVP is disgusting. If you burn it, throw it away. There is no hope of redemption.

Chow mein

Carved carrots, this really is a small detail that transforms the dish and takes very little time. Simply take a carrot and score it lengthways from top to bottom. The end of the potato peeler, ordianrily used to remove blemishes is a good tool for this. Or, hold the whole carrot down and cut grooves into it lengthways. Either of these actions will mean that when the carrot is sliced thinly, widthways, instead of coin shapes, there are little flowers.

In EL PIANO we only use primary ingredients. One of the reasons we don't have noodles on our menu often is because we don't bring any compound products into the building. This dish, which is essentially vegetables in a thickened savoury sauce served on a bed of crispy noodles, is possible for us because we make the noodles ourselves. You can skip this step by sourcing your own.

You will need the following:

> 1 chunkily cut red onion
> 1 coarsley chopped bunch of spring onions/scallions
> 1 chunkily cut red pepper
> 2 carved carrots - see the sidebar
> 16 quartered button mushrooms
> 1 large head of brocolli cut into florets
> 30g thinly sliced fresh ginger
> 200ml tamari
> 300ml water
> Scant sunflower oil or similar (not olive oil!) for sauté
> 1 TBL cornflour/cornstarch - use more for a thicker sauce

- Mix the ginger, tamari, water, cornflour/cornstarch in a jug.
- Set aside.
- Sauté all the veg in the oil until just beyond raw, about 3-5 minutes. Reduce the heat.
- Add the contents of the jug, and stir to avoid lumps.
- Pour over your choice of crispy or soft noodles
- Garnish with chopped greenery and serve.

Cheating lasagna

The cost of gluten-free pasta is often four times that of the wheat based product. So we devised this version of lasagna on the grounds that no-one looks that closely when the dish is presented, and the taste is fantastic.

This is one of those recipes that is easy to expand. Preheat the oven to medium heat and oil a good sized baking dish.

Make the 'cheesy' sauce:

> 4 TBL extra virgin olive oil
> 5 TBL rice flour
> 1L rice mylk or other plant mylk
> 1½ TBL mustard
> 250ml white wine
> 1½ tsp salt ½ tsp black pepper
> 150g nutritional yeast

- Heat the oil in a pan.
- Remove it from the heat and stir in the rice flour so that the flour is well coated by the oil.
- Return to the heat and add the mylk and nutritional yeast.
- Stir constantly until the sauce thickens.
- Stir in the mustard, wine, pepper and salt. Set aside.

Assemble the lasagna:

> 300g sliced mushrooms
> 200g well chopped fresh spinach
> 750g tomatoes whizzed with 4 cloves of fresh garlic and ½ tsp salt
> 300g polenta mixed with 2 TBL oregano
> 250ml any wine
> 2 TBL extra virgin olive oil
> black pepper or ground paprika to garnish

- Layer the ingredients into the dish. Start with the tomato so that the lasagna doesn't stick to the pan.
- Now a thin layer of the polenta-oregano mix, then the sliced mushrooms, more thin polenta-oregano, then the spinach, and so on until you run out of ingredients. We find that using ⅓ of the cheesy sauce in the middle of the dish and reserving ⅔ for the top, is best. End with the cheesy sauce.
- Create space at the corners of the dish for the wine to be poured in evenly. This, plus the fluid from the raw vegetables, will ensure the veg and polenta cook fully.
- Bake in a medium oven, about 30-40 minutes, until the top is browned. Garnish with black pepper or paprika and serve.

Satay skewers

A peanut allergy is among the most deadly, and all too often affects children before they even know they have the allergy.

In EL PIANO we use toasted broad beans aka habas fritas to provide the nutty flavour.

Do beware packaging that suggests that the beans are packaged in factories that pack peanuts. For some people the allergy is so severe that even someone breathing on them, who had peanuts the previous day and still has residue in their teeth, can cause a violent reaction.

The skewers require simply a job of assembly and always take a great deal longer than one might think. Tofu can be used instead of tempeh but is more fragile. Bamboo or metal skewers can be used interchangeably. Metal skewers conduct heat and so the cooking time is reduced. Make sure that the length of the chosen skewers will fit the cooking vessel to be used.

Prepare the satay sauce:

>4 tsp coconut sugar
>200g roasted, salted broad beans aka habas fritas
>100g dessicated coconut
>4 minced red chillies
>200ml sunflower oil or similar light salad oil
>700ml water

- *Whizz together and set aside.*

Prepare the skewers. For 4 people, each having 6 skewers, you will need:

>2 chunky chopped peppers of any colour
>1 sliced red onion
>2 sliced white onions
>24 button mushrooms
>500g tempeh cut and sliced into chunky squares larger than a postage stamp
>1 peeled and sliced pineapple
>1 green courgette

- *Thread the chopped vegetable pieces of uniform size and of contrasting colours onto the skewers. Use the onions as your 'stoppers' at the end of the skewer.*
- *Cook the skewers on the barbeque or on a griddle, turning them as they brown.*
- *Remove and serve with the satay sauce.*

Berenjenas bangkok

Deadly nightshade has four close cousins: potato, tomato, peppers and aubergine. If you are allergic to one, there is a chance you may become intolerant or allergic to the others. Just be aware.

Fresh garlic in oil is best kept in the fridge. Anaerobic bacteria can make their home in garlic. If ingested raw it can make the eater quite unwell. Any pastes or sauces with raw garlic in, make sure you cook them first rather than, as we have done, spread them on toast directly from the jar.

Aubergines are plentiful in southern Spain where this dish was devised. Harvest one, and the next day there are three more. It's much more expensive choice to make this dish in northern Europe where supply is either from a long way away or expensively produced under glass. To save expense this can also be made with half aubergine and half potatoes.

Make the Thai red curry paste by whizzing the following together in a calibrated jug:

> ¼ cup chopped red chillies
> ¼ cup coconut sugar
> ¼ cup fresh chopped garlic
> ¼ cup sunflower oil or similar light salad oil

- Set aside and enjoy noting how the colour deepens in time. You may not need all of this, so jar and refrigerate for use in future dishes.

Now for the main meal:

> 4 large aubergines, about 1K, sliced into short sticks
> 2 TBL coconut sugar
> 4 TBL tamari
> 2 TBL water
> 1 cup/60g chopped fresh basil
> Juice of 1 lime

- Mix the water, tamari and coconut sugar together in a jug. Set aside.
- Choose a deep frying pan or wok with a lid and heat to hot-hot.
- Fry 4 TBL of the red curry paste, taking care not to burn it.
- Add the chopped aubergine, stir, reduce the heat to low and cover.
- Check every 5 minutes on the aubergines. They need to be cooked fully - soft and brown.
- Turn the heat back up and toss in the tamari, coconut sugar and water.
- The aubergines are already cooked, so it's a case of choosing how wet you want the dish. The longer you cook it, the more the liquid will evaporate.
- Remove from the heat. Add the lime juice and garnish with chopped basil. Serve.

Peruvian green sauce

Miriam who, before she retired in 2016, owned EL PIANO Málaga, created this amazing sauce. All of the fire in it is from the garlic...

Whizz together this simple high-protein sauce and set aside:

> *200g tofu*
> *100ml soya mylk*
> *1 entire bunch of chopped, fresh coriander*
> *10 cloves of fresh garlic*
> *1 tsp salt and 1 tsp lime juice*

Refried beans

Traditionally fried in pig fat, our version is virtually fat-free. Watch out for beans in salted water. You may need less salt.

> *2 x 400g tins borlotti or pinto beans*
> *1 coarsely cut white onion*
> *4 TBL tomato paste*
> *2 tsp ground cumin and 1 tsp salt*

- *Whizz all and serve hot or cold.*

Cuban beans

> *400g black beans, ideally soaked in water overnight. If not, soak the beans in boiling water while preparing everything else*
> *1 diced white onion*
> *1 diced green pepper*
> *1 glass of white wine*
> *3 cloves minced garlic*
> *1 TBL oregano*
> *1 TBL extra virgin olive oil*
> *2 tsp salt*

- *Sauté the onion, pepper and garlic in the olive oil.*
- *Drain the beans and add them, and everything else.*
- *Add water so the beans are barely covered.*
- *Cover and cook slowly either on the stove, adding water as needed, in the oven or use a slow cooker. The beans are ready when they are soft and the liquid is fully absorbed.*

Álbondigas roberto

In about 2010 we stopped doing our 'meat'balls, sausages, chorizo etc with soya products. We rely instead on the amazing capacity of mushrooms and aubergines to absorb flavour and provide a deep, substantial texture.

This is a bit of 'belt and braces' as far as flavour is concerned, as it contains fresh fennel, fennel seeds as well as basil....so if you find you are short of one of these ingredients, the overall flavour will still come through.

Make the tomato sauce first:

> 1 K fresh cherry tomatoes
> 1 TBL fennel seeds
> 3 TBL olive oil
> 40g of chopped fresh basil
> 1 tsp salt

- In a covered pan, on a medium heat, cook everything together, except the basil, until the tomatoes are soft.
- Set aside and keep warm.

Now for the "meat"balls. Pre-heat the oven to medium heat and prepare an oiled baking tray:

> 2K mushrooms - any sort will do
> 2 heads of chopped fresh fennel
> 300g tomato paste
> 200ml extra virgin olive oil
> 80g chopped fresh basil
> 300-400g chickpea flour aka besan, gram or garbanzo bean flour
> 1½ - 2 TBL salt

- Heat the oil in a pan and add the mushrooms, fennel, salt, and tomato paste.
- Cover and cook until the veg have 'cooked down' and their juices are evident. Bear in mind that veg vary. Fresh firm mushrooms will leach out more fluid than older dryer ones.
- Give it all a whizz, choosing how much texture you want the mix to have.
- Add the fresh basil and then the flour little by little. You want a wet mix, nothing too doughy.
- Form into balls and place on the oiled oven tray. Don't worry if they appear flat. It's better to roll them after they cook than to have a floury result.
- Bake for 30 minutes or until the balls are firm.
- Remove and serve topped with the TOMATO SAUCE and chopped basil.

Carimex

A fusion of Caribbean and Mexican flavours, the sweet of the Caribbean plantain and the smokey of the Latin American chipotle sauce is balanced by the good old plain potato, itself also a native of the New World. Once you have the sauce, it's a fast dish to reproduce and the sauce can be used in a host of other dishes. Everything needs to be at hand, ready to throw in the pan for a final furious and frenetic stir fry of a mere 3-4 minutes. Ideal for a dinner party, CariMex has the advantage of drama, colour, speed plus the option of previous preparation.

Make a cheating chipotle sauce first:

Whizz together

> ⅓ cup sunflower oil
> ⅓ cup coconut sugar
> 125g fresh red chillies
> ⅓ cup water
> ¼ tsp salt
> 1½ tsp liquid smoke
> 1 tsp lime juice

- Bring everything to the boil except the smoke and lime juice.
- Stir continuously for 8 minutes.
- Remove from the heat and add the smoke and lime juice.
- Whizz and set aside.

Per person served you will need:

> ½ plantain, sliced
> 4-6 big chunks of cold pre-boiled potatoes
> 1 diced spring onion/scallion
> 2 TBL chopped fresh coriander/cilantro
> dash of sunflower or any light salad oil.
> ¼ tsp salt

- Heat to hot-hot a dash of the oil in a deep frying pan or wok.
- Toss in the plaintain and potato. Ideally 1 serving at a time.
- As the plantain and potato brown, throw on the chipotle sauce to taste. A guide would be 1 TBL per serving.
- Toss a further minute. Remove from the heat.
- Toss in a bowl with the onion, fresh herb and salt to taste.
- Serve.

In the restaurant we serve this with cornbread, the recipe for which is in our BREADS section, on p. 42.

"Meat"loaf & gravy

We use cherry tomatoes and inevitably some of them remain, if not whole, then at least recognisable. Little domes of red peeping through make the dish textured to taste and festive to look at.

Disaster management for the gravy: if it goes lumpy, simply remove from the heat at the end and give it all a good whizz.

Pre-heat the oven to medium heat. Oil an oven tray with extra virgin olive oil. The benefit of the flat tray, as opposed to a loaf pan, is that even slices are guaranteed. There is no danger of them falling apart due to gravity.

For the "meat"loaf:

> 5 cups chopped portobello mushrooms
> 2½ cups whole ripe tomatoes
> 2½ cups chopped leeks
> 1 TBL chopped fresh sage
> 2 tsp salt and 1 tsp black pepper
> ½ cup quinoa
> 1 cup rice flour - more if needed
> ¼ cup extra virgin olive oil

- Put the oil in a large pan and gently cook the mushrooms, tomatoes, leeks, sage, salt and pepper until the fluid has escaped the tomatoes and mushrooms and the mix is wet.
- Whizz half of it, leaving the rest coarse.
- Remove from the heat and add the quinoa and flour, enough to hold the mix together but not so much that it is claggy.
- Flatten into the oven tray and bake 30 minutes or until solid. Cut into squares and serve - instant slices!

The gravy is embarassingly easy...

> ½ large or 1 small chopped onion
> 1½ TBL extra virgin olive oil
> 4 TBL of any flour you like - we use buckwheat flour
> 1L vegetable stock or water
> 4 TBL yeast extract

- Sauté the onion in the oil until browned.
- Remove from the heat and stir in the flour, allowing it to absorb all of the oil.
- Add the fluid and the yeast extract and return to the heat, stirring constantly until it thickes, about 5-10 minutes. A richer gravy will result if some red wine is used as part of the fluid.

In the restaurant we serve this with violetta heritage breed potatoes. They are one of the few non-white potatoes not to loose their colour when cooked. A great pile of purple! And the flavour is out of this world.

150

Roast veg

This is a wonderfully colourful dish and we usually have a few trays for the annual staff party.

What's astounding every year is that we can never make enough roast veg and people who come, who are less than keen on the idea of EL PIANO food, always say how much they like them.

This is so simple we almost didn't put it in the book. Wrong thinking. Simple tasty dishes that are easy to prepare and cook while you do something else is just what many of us need. For a crispier result parboil the veg to reduce the starch.

Choose colourful vegetables such as

> *potatoes and sweet potatoes*
> *peppers, red, green, yellow, orange*
> *red and white onions*
> *carrots, parsnips and beetroot*

- *Chop them any size, as long as they are about the same size.*
- *Put them on oven trays, no more than two pieces deep.*
- *Pour on 100ml olive oil and 1 TBL per tray and toss the veg well.*
- *Roast in a medium oven until the hardest (usually the potato) are soft. Serve.*

Puerros al sésamo

Two ingredients and the most sensational taste...

Choose fresh, stiff, crisp leeks, ideally with the roots still on

> *4 large leeks*
> *4 TBL toasted sesame paste aka tahini - toasted is the darker version and has a stronger, nuttier taste*

- *Put a pan of water to boil.*
- *Cut the leeks lengthways in four, stopping just short of the roots. Now it is easy to wash them under the tap to remove any grit without them all falling apart.*
- *Remove the root end and cut them across so that you have finger lengths.*
- *Throw them in the boiling water for just 5 minutes. Remove, drain and put them in your serving dish.*
- *Stir in the tahini.*
- *Serve.*

This can be a main meal when accompanied by a choice of fritters and salad.

6
Sauces

Red lead

The term 'square meal' probably came from the Navy where, years ago, many people joined up because at least they would be fed. The food was served on compartmentalised trays, hence the term 'square meal'. However, some say the food was so bad that it was inedible without being plastered in 'red lead' aka tomato ketchup.

This will yield ketchup to fill a 300ml bottle.

50g tomato paste
50ml extra virgin olive oil - no other!
50ml cider or white wine vinegar
1 small diced white onion
2 cloves of fresh garlic
100ml water
½ tsp ground English mustard
½ tsp ground nutmeg
½ tsp ground cumin
½ tsp ground cinnamon
½ tsp black pepper
½ tsp salt

- Whizz everything together and cook on medium-high heat 12 minutes, stirring constantly.
- Cool, pour into a lidded container and refrigerate. It will last many weeks (if not devoured!)

Rhaita

This classic from the Indian sub-continent is a fantastic accompaniment for fritters as it balances the grease and, when served with curries, can cool the palate! Variations for this sauce can be chopped mint instead of cucumber, vinegar instead of lemon juice, and some cooks also add finely chopped onions.

150ml pure soya milk, just beans and water, any additives and stabilisers and it simply won't work
¼ cucumber, grated
juice of 1 lemon
¼ tsp salt
¼ tsp pepper

- Whizz the mylk and lemon juice -it will thicken slightly.
- Fold in the cucumber - there are two ways to use the cucumber (1) simply add it, fluid and all, and have a thinner rhaita or (2) squeeze out the excess moisture by hand from the grated cucumber and add it making for a thicker rhaita.

Mayo

While there is plenty of fat in this recipe, there are certainly no cholesterol inducing animal products.

For those you know who are not so keen on eliminating animal products from their diet, yet are at risk of cholesterol associated diseases, this is a win win. In EL PIANO we put it in the category of products that we label 'they will never know'.

If anyone you know loves mayo and eats loads of it, just start serving this...

It's a bit of a party trick, and we learned it from Roberto García. You do need a hand or stick blender. Mayonnaise is an emulsion where the two fluids, oil and mylk, are held in suspension. The amount you make is up to you. This recipe is entirely proportional and can be scaled up or down as long as the ratio, 1 measure of soya mylk to 3 measures of oil, is adhered to.

> 1 cup of pure soya mylk
>> it cannot contain stabilisers, additives, sweeteners or vitamins, or the mayo will not work - check the container, it should simply contain hulled soya beans and water, and, ideally be organic
>
> 3 cups of sunflower oil - you can use olive oil but we find the flavour too strong
> juice of 1 lemon
> ½ tsp black pepper (optional)
> ½ tsp salt

- Whizz the mylk adding the oil evenly - we've seen people throw the oil and the mylk together all at once, and still get the right result, but it is less risky, and easier to create the suspension of fluids, if you go at it gently. Be sure, if using a stick blender, rather than a beater, that you move it up and down to let in the air.
- During the adding of the final cup of oil the mylk will begin to thicken noticably.
- Add the salt and lemon.
- If you prefer the mayo less thick, simply add more soya mylk to the desired consistency.

Variations are many. Not only can you add curry powder for the 'coronation chicken' mayo, garlic for 'ali oli' and tomato paste for the 'shrimp cocktail' flavour, our mayo will also transform readily into sweet creams for cakes and puddings. A dash of vanilla, some citrus zest and a touch of brandy or cinnamon, nutmeg and syrup are all that is needed... it's up to you.

Coconut creams

The discard from the coconut tins, the 'whey' for want of a better description, can be added to curries r drinks.

Coconut products vary wildly in colour and texture and in the proportion that is cream, as opposed to the 'whey'.

Try out different brands until you find one that you like. Remember that coconut quality will vary from harvest to harvest and so you may need to change brands from year to year.

This recipe is proportional and the quantities can be adjusted to make as much or as little as is needed.

> 350g coconut cream - this is awkward to predict since the coconut milk in any tin varies from tin to tin. You just need to keep opening them and scraping out the cream until there is 350g
> ¼ cup of syrup
> the zest from ½ orange
> pinch of salt
> 2 tsp cinnamon
> ½ tsp vanilla

- Whisk everything together in a bowl by hand, not machine. Mechanical devices can cause the coconut to semi-curdle and become grainy.

The above is the recipe we use for the cream served with our carrot cake. To develop your own creams, just substitute your own flavours.

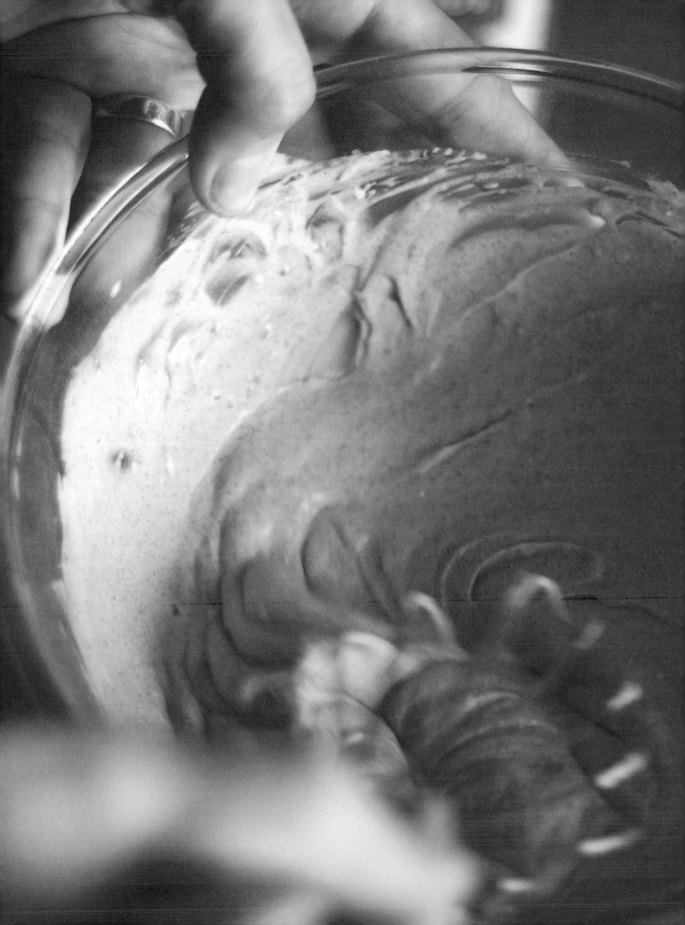

Toffee sauces

Dates are so sweet that our first toffee sauce has no added sugar... but that does not mean that it is sugar-free. Far from it. Sugars have varying properties and impact the body in different ways, cane sugar perhaps being the most damaging. So take care when serving people who have diabetes and make sure that you are clear in what you claim about any ingredients.

These recipes are proportional and the quantities can be adjusted to make as much or as little as is needed.

For a date based sauce you will need:

> 2½ cups of dried, stoned dates
> 500ml rice mylk
> 1 tsp vanilla
> 1 tsp salt

- Heat on a low heat until the dates have softened.
- Whizz and serve hot. warm or cold.

For a coconut based sauce you will need:

> 100ml sunflower oil
> 200g coconut sugar
> 1 x 400g tin/can of well mixed coconut milk - the cream and the 'whey' together
> ½ tsp vanilla
> ½ tsp salt

- Heat the oil in a pan, medium to low heat.
- Add the coconut sugar until it starts to melt, adding the coconut milk to reduce the heat so that sugar doesn't burn.
- Add the salt and vanilla and bring to the boil.
- Simmer for 5 minutes and remove from the heat.
- Use hot, warm or cold.

Any excess toffee sauce can be used as a syrup for shakes and smoothies.

7
Pickles, Chutneys & Relishes

Cranberry relish

Both of these recipes come from the Cherokee part of Bob's family. (The Cheyenne part were terrible cooks and lived on boiled beans, doughnuts and vodka...)

A very simple, yet exquisite, seasonal relish using fresh cranberries.

500g fresh cranberries
an equal volume of peeled fresh oranges
coconut sugar to taste

- *Whizz together adjusting the sugar as required.*
- *Leave to rest for at least an hour so that the flavours fuse.*

Dill pickle

Another simple pickle that will keep in or out of the refrigerator, although its longevity is assured when kept cool.

12 thinly sliced fresh cucumbers
3 thinly sliced fresh white onions
250ml water
500g coconut sugar
250ml white wine or cider vinegar
1 TBL dried dill or 4 stalks of fresh diced dillweed
1 tsp salt

- *Put the onions and cucumber in a large bowl and find a lid that will cover it - even an inverted tray will do.*
- *Boil the water, sugar, vinegar, salt and dill.*
- *Dump the boiling fluid over the onions and cucumber and cover immediately.*
- *When the mixture has cooled, store in covered jars or boxes.*

Tomato chutney

To store this chutney you will need refrigeration. The idea is to make it easy for people to use up excess crops, or take advantage of low prices at the market.

To store without refrigeration, bottling techniques are simple but require some investment.

Use lever clip bottling jars (not screw top jars) like the one shown on p.171. Put the chutney into each jar up to the mark indicated on the jar. Clip the jar closed.

Submerge the jars in a deep pan of cold water. Bring to the boil. Bubbles escape from the jars as the heat creates a vaccuum. Cook 5 minutes or until the bubbles cease. Remove from the pan and allow to cool naturally.

Once cold, test that a vaccuum has formed by removing the clip. The glass lid will stay on!

This is a great way to use up all of the tomatoes at the end of the season, whatever their colour... Like the Autumn Fruit Chutney on p.174, the recipe is designed to encourage us to make chutney by using whatever weights there are to hand. We refer to the fruit you have to hand as X.

X K of tomatoes
½ X of coconut sugar
¼ X peeled and chopped onions
¼ X of vinegar, either white wine vinegar or a more astringent apple cider vinegar
¼ X of chopped dates (optional)
$^1/_{16}$ X paprika - there are three principal sorts of paprika available: sweet, smoked and spicy. You choose.

- Throw everything in a deep pan and cook on a gentle heat until the tomatoes break up. The volume will reduce by about one third.
- Refrigerate in sealed containers, be they glass jars or plastic boxes.
- The chutney will keep in the refrigerator almost indefinitely.

As with any chutney the flavours can be altered to taste, as can the sweetener and vinegar content. Be mindful that sweeteners and vinegars are two of the four additives for preserving, the other two being salt and alcohol. The more the 'water' is boiled off, the higher the sweet and acid content. It is the higher levels of acid and sugars that prolong the keeping quality of the chutney.

Lime pickle

Most lime pickle recipes call for the limes to be quartered or halved. That works well in countries where limes grow and can be relied upon to be fat and juicy.

Far too many limes sold in Northern Europe are small and dry. By slicing them it is easier to extract their juices, vital for a good result.

In general the 'rules' for using oil are as follows: Oriental and Asian cooking, NO olive oil. Middle Eastern and Mediterranean dishes, YES to olive oil.

This lime pickle recipe is one of the exceptions.

This is a pickle really worth the wait. Like almost all of the EL PIANO recipes it can be adjusted to make it your own. For example, the store bought lime pickles are often unbearably spicey, and the citrus that is so good for palate cleansing is overpowered. Decide how piquante you want it and adjust the spices accordingly. The recipe below is for a mild result with much greater focus on flavour than on heat. Don't be tempted to add fresh garlic as garlic attracts anaerobic bacteria which can become hazardous when products are stored.

16 sliced limes
1 red chilli, at least 10cm long, split lengthways
½ cup coconut sugar
½ cup salt
1 TBL ground turmeric
1 TBL whole fenugreek seeds
1 TBL whole coriander seed
1L extra virgin olive oil - more or less
20 green olives (optional)

- *Crush the whole spices by hand either in a bag under a rolling pin or wine bottle, or with mortar and pestle.*
- *Combine the spices with the sliced limes, the whole chilli and the salt.*
- *Jar into a lever lid jar as shown in the photo, and close it.*
- *Keep for about 3 weeks in full light, but not full sun. A windowsill is ideal, turning it and inverting it daily to keep the salt and spices moving through the lime slices. The limes will soften, including the peel, and the juices will be drawn out by the salt and spices.*
- *When you are happy that the limes and their peel are soft, remove from the jar and discard the saline fluid.*
- *Rinse the jar and pack in the limes, chilli and spices. Add the green olives if you wish.*
- *Cover with olive oil and store.*
- *It is ready to use in 1 week, and, because it does not contain fresh garlic, will keep almost indefinitely.*

Mango chutney

Chutney is a Hindi word which means 'good to eat' and became part of British, and then world, cuisine as a result of Britian's long asscoiation with India.

During the British raj the colonials discovered ginger as a means to increase the speed of horses. Rammed up the rectum of a horse the burning sensation makes them go faster. Hence the origins in British English of 'Gee up neddy' and 'Gee gee' as baby language for horse.

This has to be the queen of chutneys...

To make 6 x 500ml jars you will need:

> *3K peeled and stoned mangoes (probably 5K of whole fruit)*
> *1½K coconut sugar*
> *1½K chopped white onions*
> *200g grated garlic*
> *200g grated ginger*
> *1 tsp each of whole cumin, coriander, green cardomom, and cloves*
> *1 tsp each of ground cayenne pepper and turmeric*
> *750ml white wine vinegar (apple cider vinegar is too harsh)*

- Leave the mangoes and the coconut sugar together in a deep, stainless steel pan, not aluminium, overnight.
- The following day gently heat the mango and coconut sugar and add the ground spices.
- Toast the whole spices by dry-frying them and add to the pan.
- Finally add the vinegar.
- Cook slowly for about 3 hours or until the chutney thickens and tester drops set on a cool surface.
- Pour into the jars and seal.

Faux mango chutney

Mangoes are costly in Northern Europe, and, if you think about it, what makes mango chutney so delicious is as much the spices as the fruit. We have used pears, greengages and yellow plums to produce lovely chutneys that blend the local autumn harvests with far-away exotic spices. The key is the soft pulp of the fruit (hence apples are not so good) and the light colours of the skins. The advantage is that there is less waste (mango stones are huge!) and no peeling is necessary.

Autumn fruit chutney

This is a recipe that does rely on refrigeration. The idea is to make it simple so that people can use up excess crops, or take advantage of low prices at the market.

To store without refrigeration, bottling techniques are easy, but require some investment.

Use lever clip bottling jars (not screw top jars) as shown on page 171. Put the chutney into each jar up to the mark indicated on the jar. Clip the jar closed.

Submerge the jars in a deep pan of cold water. Bring to the boil. Bubbles escape from the jars as the heat creates a vaccuum. Cook 5 minutes or until the bubbles cease. Remove from the pan and allow to cool naturally. Once the jar is cold, test that a vaccuum has formed by removing the clip. The glass lid will stay on!

This is a great way to use up ALL the apples and pears at the end of the season whatever state they are in. The recipe is designed to encourage us to make chutney by using the weights there are to hand. We can never know how much the neighbours will give us, or what weight any windfall apples or city harvest fruits will be. We refer to the fruit you have to hand as X.

X K of apples and pears
½ X of coconut sugar
¼ X peeled and chopped onions
¼ X of vinegar, either white wine viengar or apple cider vinegar which is more astringent
¼ X of raisins (optional)
$^1/_{16}$ X cinnamon
$^1/_{16}$ X whole coriander seeds.

- Throw everything in a deep pan - we mean everything... No peeling or coring, no need even to chop, although it does speed the cooking if the fruit is in smaller pieces.
- Cook covered and on a gentle heat until the fruits break up. The weight will be the same, but the volume is reduced by as much as one third.
- Refrigerate in sealed containers, be they glass jars or plastic boxes.
- The chutney will keep in the refrigerator almost indefinitely.

As with any chutney the flavours can be altered to taste, as can the sweetener and vinegar content. Be mindful that sweeteners and vinegars are two of the four additives for preserving, the other two being salt and alcohol. The more the 'water' is boiled off, the higher the sweet and acid content. It is the higher levels of acid and sugars that prolong the keeping quality of the chutney.

8
Desserts

Tiramisu

This is Bob's absolute favourite EL PIANO dessert of all time. When we were working to put this book together he said more than once that he hoped that, if people made only one recipe from the book, then it would be the tiramisu.

In the restaurant we make this with brewed coffee but the recipe is so fiddly Bob thought it would be more merciful to suggest to make it with instant coffee for the cookbook.

Bake the sponge:

> 1 cup buckwheat flour
> ⅓ cup of syrup
> ⅓ cup of sunflower oil
> ⅔ cup of coconut mylk drink
> 1 tsp vanilla
> ½ tsp salt
> 1½ TBL baking powder

- Whip together the oil, vanilla and sweetener - then the mylk.
- Fold in the flour, salt and baking powder.
- Bake in an oven tray at medium heat, 15-20 minutes or until the sponge is set. Remove and set to cool.

Make the soak sauce by combining:

> 2 TBL instant coffee
> 300ml hot water
> 2 TBL cocoa
> 100ml syrup
> ¼ tsp salt
> 60ml brandy - check the brandy is vegan. Many aren't!

Make the coconut cream:

> 500g coconut cream - this is awkward to predict since coconut milk varies from tin to tin. You just need to keep opening them and scraping out the cream until there is 500g
> 40ml brandy
> 40ml vanilla essence
> 80ml syrup
> ¼ tsp salt

- Whip everything by hand - not machine!

Now assemble it:

- Put a drop of brandy in the base of each parfait dish.
- Slice the cake into fingers and briefly soak in the soak sauce, just a quick in and out.
- Repeatedly layer the soaked cake and the coconut cream into the parfait glasses finishing on a cream layer.
- Dust with cocoa and refrigerate, at least 2 hours.

Elaina's ginger bread

Elaina made this traditional ginger bread for years, long before she was asked to make it vegan, as well free of refined sugar, gluten and palm oil.

The point of mentioning this is to encourage you to adapt any of your favourite recipes.

Eggs in cakes are unnecessary - baking powder will given them lift.

Sunflower oil will work instead of solid fats in just about anything, including icings!

Buckwheat flour is a fantastic flour for cakes, best used when baking cakes with strong flavours. Chocolate, for example, and cinnamon as another example, will mask the flavour of buckwheat for those who are less keen.

Maize flour , a very finely milled yellow corn flour, also doubles as a cake flour.

Pre-heat the oven to just above medium heat. Prepare a standard loaf pan or 15cm square tin.

You will need:

150ml sunflower oil
75g coconut sugar
3 TBL syrup
2 heaped TBL marmalade, sugar-free is available
200ml soya mylk
225g buckwheat flour
½ tsp salt
1 tsp bicarbonate of soda
1 tsp baking powder
4 tsp heaped ground ginger

- Heat all the wet ingredients until the coconut sugar has melted, taking care not to let the mix boil.
- Sieve the dry ingredients to ensure that there are no lumps and that they are well blended.
- Combine the wet with the dry and pour into the tin.
- Bake for 45 minutes, turn out, allow to cool and then serve.

Fresh fruit cake

Another version of fresh fruit cake is an unbaked cake of fresh, juicy fruits layered with polenta.

We made this in EL PIANO many years ago but it's not well suited to restaurant trade as it dries out too rapidly. However if you are having an event and you are reasonably certain the cake will all be eaten, we can recommend it.

Using a silicone cake mould or a spring clip cake mould, build up a cake of layers of squashed fresh fruit and polenta soaked in fruit juice and flavoured with vanilla.

Let the cake stand overnight, remove the collar of the mould and serve.

A fantastic addition to any summer table as this recipe especially lends itself to the use of summer berries.

Pre-heat the oven to medium. Oil and flour a 1500ml cake tin or mould.

You will need:

> ½ cup coconut sugar OR ½ cup syrup
> ½ cup sunflower oil
> 1¼ coconut mylk drink OR, if using syrup, 1 cup mylk
> ½ tsp vanilla
> ½ tsp salt
> 1½ cups buckwheat flour
> 1½ tsp baking powder
> 250g mixed berries for the cake and 250g mixed berries for the decoration

- Mix together the sweetener, mylk, oil, vanilla and salt.
- Fold in the flour, followed by the baking powder.
- Finally fold in 250g of fresh fruit. Work quickly as the baking powder becomes active as soon as it hits the liquid.
- Scrape the mixture into the chosen tin or mould, then place the mould in the oven as soon as possible.
- Check the cake after 20 minutes. The cake is baked when a knife inserted in the centre comes out clean.
- Wait 10 minutes before turning out.
- Decorate with the remaining 250g fresh fruit.

Brownies

A classic staple of
the vegan dessert
repertoire this
recipe is open to
many variations

Swap out the oil
for avocadoes or
peanut butter...

Swap in fava
bean flour or
buckwheat flour
for the green pea
flour. We have even
made a variety in
EL PIANO that
contained green
peas, much to the
amazement of
many.

Ditch the plant
mylks in favour of
fruit juices or even
water.

Provided you
stick to the basic
formula for fat,
fluid and flour, you
cannot go too far
wrong with this
recipe.
As it's a brownie, it
almost doesn't even
matter if it doesn't
rise.

Pre-heat the oven to medium heat and oil a 1500ml cake tin.
If made from silicone no oiling is required after the first use.

Make the chocolate sauce:

> 300ml water
> 250ml/350g syrup
> 150g cocoa powder
> ½ tsp vanilla
> ½ tsp salt
> more sweetener to taste

- Put everything in a pan.
- Heat gently to 85°, in other words less than boiling, as it is
  easy to burn. Set aside.

Bake the brownie:

> 35g cocoa powder
> 200g coconut sugar
> 220g green pea flour
> 250ml plant mylk
> 250ml sunflower oil
> 1 tsp baking powder
> ½ tsp vanilla
> ½ tsp salt
> sunflower oil for oiling the tin

- Mix the dry ingredients.
- Add the wet ingredients and mix well and mix quickly so as
  not to exhaust the baking powder.
- Pour into the greased mould and bake for 20-25 minutes or
  until a knife comes out clean.
- Remove, cool and then serve topped with the chocolate
  sauce.

Lemon drizzle cake

If you like a tangy-er, less sweet cake, don't hesitate to reduce the sweetener and increase the lemon. Using lemon zest gives a more penetrating citrus flavour.

Pre-heat the oven to medium. Oil and flour a 1500ml cake tin or mould.

For the drizzle:

> 75ml lemon juice (usually 1½ lemons)
> 3 TBL coconut sugar
> 50ml syrup

- Mix together and set aside.

For the cake:

> ½ cup coconut sugar or ½ cup syrup
> ½ cup sunflower oil
> 1¼ coconut mylk drink or, if using syrup, 1 cup mylk
> 1 tsp vanilla
> ½ tsp salt
> 1½ cups buckwheat flour
> 1½ tsp baking powder
> zest of 1 lemon

- Mix together the sweetener, mylk, oil, vanilla, lemon zest and salt.
- Fold in the flour, followed by the baking powder. Remember to work quickly as the baking powder begins working as soon as it hits the liquid.
- Scrape the mixture into the chosen tin or mould, then into the oven as soon as possible.
- Check the cake after 20 minutes. The cake is baked when a knife inserted in the centre comes out clean.
- Wait 10 minutes before turning out and spoon the drizzle sauce over the top while the cake is still warm.

Chia seed delight

Elena devised this recipe a few years ago when chia seeds were the darling of the vegan kitchen. We were completely smitten!

While chia may have reduced in popularity and is less common on menus now than it was, the miraculousness of the chia seeds never ceases to amaze us. They swell and absorb the coconut resulting in the lightest of desserts with a subtle fragrant flavour.

You only need three ingredients:

> 1 full tin of coconut milk
> ¼ cup chia seeds
> ¼ cup syrup

- Combine everything in a bowl.
- Use a hand whisk to eliminate any lumps.
- Divide evenly between 4 fancy glass containers.

To make a coulis topping:

> use either dried fruit or fresh.

- For dried fruit, cover the fruit with boiling water, leave it to stand for about 5 minutes and then whizz to a purée.

- For fresh fruit, simply whizz the fruit to a pulp. It may be necessary to add some sweetener.

Banoffee cake

This amazing cake comes from Alice's home repertoire and has been very popular on the menu.

A classic flavour combination of banana and toffee, the clever use of bananas in the cake mix obviates the need for any added sweeteners.

Make the toffee sauce:

> 50ml sunflower oil
> 100g coconut sugar
> ½ of a 400g tin/can of well mixed coconut milk - the cream and the 'whey' together
> ¼ tsp vanilla
> ¼ tsp salt

- Heat the oil in a pan, medium to low heat.
- Add the coconut sugar until it starts to melt, adding the coconut milk to reduce the heat so the sugar doesn't burn.
- Add the salt and vanilla and bring to the boil.
- Simmer for 5 minutes and remove from the heat.
- Use hot, warm or cold.

Bake the cake:

> 4 bananas (5 if they are small, 3 if they are large) plus 2 sliced bananas for the base as well as some extra to decorate the cake. We cut the bananas for the base lengthways in order to save time...
> 500ml rice mylk
> 300g maize flour - the very finely milled yellow flour, not polenta or the white cornflour for thickening
> 1½ tsp baking powder
> ½ tsp vanilla
> ½ tsp salt
> sunflower oil for oiling the tin

- Pre-heat the oven to medium heat and oil a 1500ml cake tin. If made from silicone no oiling is required after the first use.
- Lay the 2 sliced bananas along the base of the cake tin and drizzle some of the toffee sauce over them, just to cover.
- Whizz together the 4 bananas, mylk, vanilla and salt.
- Mix in the flour taking care to beat out any lumps.
- Stir in the baking powder evenly and quickly.
- Pour into the greased mould and bake for 20-25 minutes or until a knife comes out clean.
- Remove, cool and then serve topped with more sauce. It is as good served warm nd is great with coconut creams on p.161

Carrot cake

Bob began working in EL PIANO as a child, helping fetch and carry, and then sometimes would be allowed to count coins into piles. Although not really needed, it made a 6 year old feel important!

We've had carrot cake on the menu in EL PIANO for more than 20 years and the recipe has changed as we have thrown ingredients out of the kitchen, such as refined sugar and palm oil. So, over time, the recipe has evolved into Bob's version which we use today.

The recipe will be more accessible for those who already bake cakes in that it does rely on some previous baking experience. The trouble with using any fresh veg is that you can never know exactly how much moisture, a carrot for example, will contain.

We bake it in an oven roasting tray and cut it into squares. It's easier to manage and takes less time to bake.

Pre-heat the oven to medium hot. Oil the oven roasting tray.

Fruit and veg ingredients:

> 3¾ cups of grated carrots
> zest of 1 orange
> 2½ cups of seedless raisins, less if cash is in short supply - fewer raisins won't ruin the cake

Wet ingredients:

> 200ml orange juice
> 200ml sunflower or any light salad oil
> 500ml syrup - we use a blend of carob, grape and apple

Flavourings:

> ¾ TBL salt - do it! Trust us!
> 1 TBL ground cinnamon
> 2 tsp vanilla

Dry ingredients:

> 4 cups maize flour - not corn meal, not polenta, not corn flour, this is very finely milled dried corn kernels - smooth and yellow. If you struggle to find it buckwheat flour will do
> 3 TBL of baking powder - yes, it's not a typo, you do need that much

- Mix the fruit and veg ingredients with the wet ingredients and the flavourings in a large bowl.
- Add the dry ingredients adjusting the flour as required. The mix should be stiffer than a batter but ever so slightly more fluid than a standard cake mix.
- Pour onto the oven tray and ensure an even spread.
- Bake for 30-40 minutes or until a knife inserted in the centre comes out clean.
- Cool, cut into squares and eat!

We serve this with different creams, both soya and coconut based. Have a look at the sauce section from p.154 onwards to find out more.

Cheesecakes

A welcome change from the tofu based cheesecakes, this is light and astonishingly successful as the bearer of exquisite flavours. Not to be missed.

The real trick to this recipe is kind of out of the cook's hands and is all about getting the right tin of coconut milk in order to get the right cream. You may have to experiment to find the brand and the harvest that is smooth enough yet thick enough. But once found, the possibilities are endless.

(Bob wrote this side-bar. He's obsessed with coconut quality. Can you tell?)

First make the base:

> ¾ cup quinoa, rinsed to remove any bitterness
> 200ml water
> ½ tsp salt
> 2 tsp coconut sugar
> 60g softened creamed coconut block

- Boil the quinoa in the water. when the water is gone it should be 'al dente'
- Add the rest, mix well and press into ramekins. Set aside.

Make the 'cheese' filler:

> 800g of coconut cream, extracted from tins of coconut milk. It's hard to predict how many will be needed since the proportion of cream and 'whey' in every tin varies
> Very fine zest of 8 lemons
> ¼ tsp salt
> 3½ TBL coconut sugar

- Beat the above together and divide between the ramekins.
- Leave it to set in the refrigerator - overnight is best, although, depending on the coconut quality, this can take less time.

Make the topping:

> 40g blueberries
> 1 TBL lemon juice
> 1 tsp coconut sugar

- Whizz together and divide between the ramekins just before service.

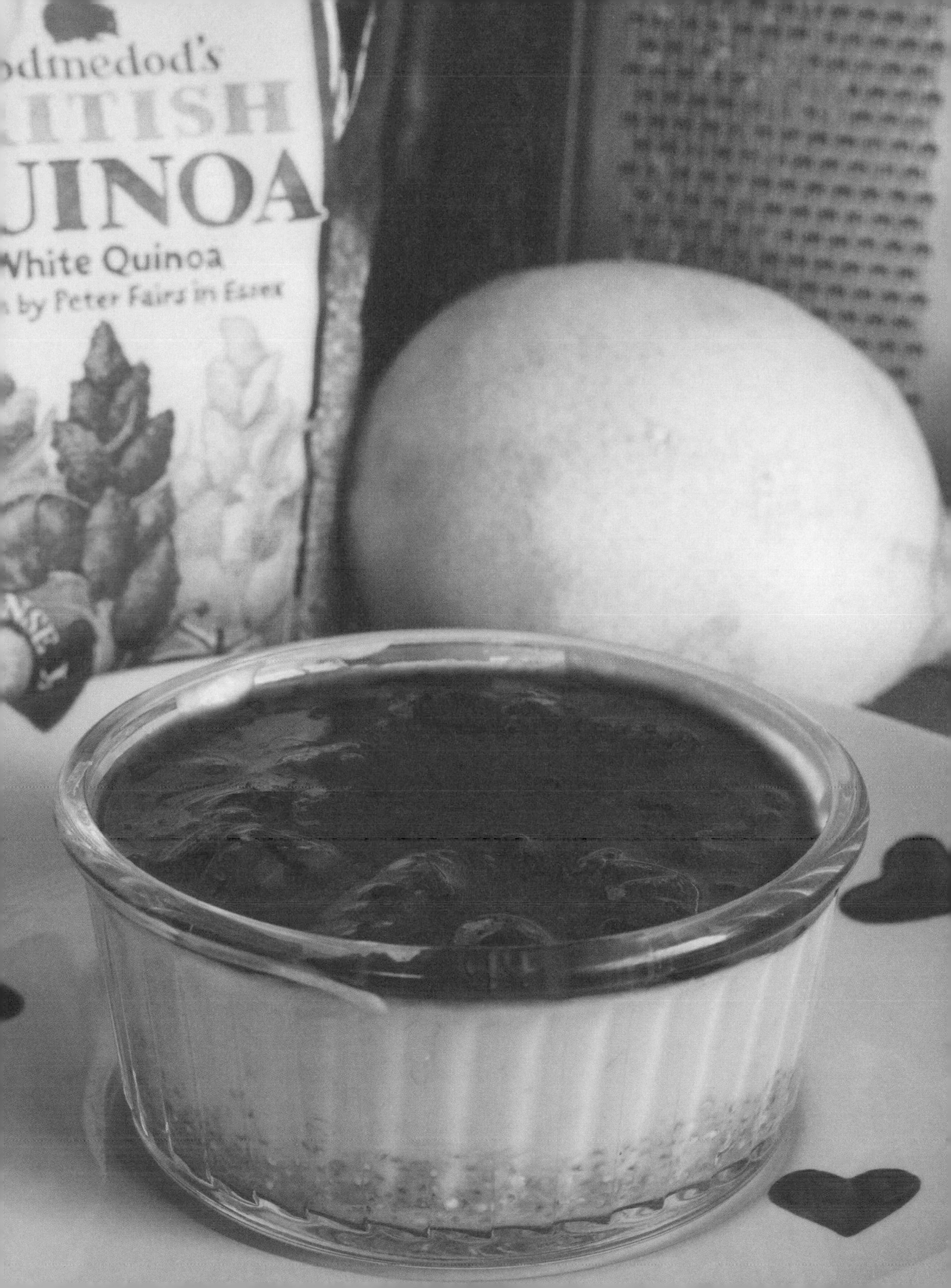
odmedod's
ITISH
JINOA
White Quinoa
n by Peter Fairs in Essex

Traditional fruit cake

Traditional, rich, fruit cakes, the type that are served in the UK at weddings and at Christmas, contain very little flour and hardly rise, so eggs are completely irrelevant.

By all means adapt your own family favourite being guided by this recipe.

Pre-heat the oven to just below medium heat. Prepare a 20cm square tin by lining it with greaseproof paper. The cake is a long time in the oven and this paper lining is designed to both protect the sides from scorch, as well as to ease its removal it from the tin.

You will need:

> 500g mixed vine fruits
> 250g sultanas
> 200g glacé cherries (optional)
> 120g coconut sugar
> 200ml syrup
> 200ml sunflower oil
> 50g coconut oil
> 300g buckwheat flour
> 2 tsp mixed spice
> ½ tsp ground nutmeg
> ¼ tsp xanthum gum - keeps the cake from crumbing
> 1½ tsp baking powder
> zest and juice of each 1 lemon and 1 orange
> 50ml of alcoholic spirits
> ½ tsp of salt

- Combine all the dried fruit with the syrup, alcohol, citrus zest and juice.
- Leave it to stand at room temperature overnight.
- Sieve the flour, spices, baking powder and xanthum gum. Set aside.
- In a separate bowl whisk together the sunflower oil, coconut oil and coconut sugar creating a creamy, light result.
- Now add a spoonful each of the sieved dry ingredients and the fruit and work them into the mix.
- Keep adding fruit and flour bit by bit until ¾ of both the flour and the fruit have been worked into the cream. Fold in the final ¼. This method helps stop all the fruit sinking to the bottom of the cake.
- Pour the mix into the lined tin and bake in the oven for 1½-2 hours. The cake is done when a knife inserted into the centre comes out clean.
- Cool and turn out of the tin. The cake will keep in an airtight container for many months. An extra option is to wrap it in an alcohol soaked cloth and then put it in the container.

Pacific paradise

Coconut is a natural thickener and with this dessert it comes into its own.

The result, when warm, is a completely light, mousse-like dessert that melts in your mouth.

When chilled it cuts easily into pie slices and will travel easily.

Just as an aside, we used to call this by it's original Indonesian street food name, poké. Didn't sell. (Reminiscent of the Nova car sales in South America where 'no va' means 'it doesn't go') So we upgraded the name to Pacific Poké. Didn't sell. Latest version, as above. So what's in a name? A lot perhaps.

No added fat and no added sugar for this dessert. No salt either!

Pre-heat the oven to medium hot. Prepare a 1500 mould by sprinkling dessicated coconut or polenta on the base to act as a crust.

All you need are three ingredients:

> 8-12 bananas
> 1 x 200g block of creamed coconut sliced into 8 pieces (in summer this will not be necessary as the coconut liquifies in warm weather)
> a pinch of cinnamon

- Peel the bananas and break them into a large bowl.
- Add boiling water so that it is just short of covering the bananas - it's not possible to give an exact amount as the size of bananas varies.
- Now add the coconut and cinnamon and whizz.
- Pour the mix over the back of your open hand and onto the chosen base. This technique helps to stop the fluid from hitting the polenta or dessicated coconut and displacing it.
- Bake for 30-40 minutes or until a knife inserted in the centre comes out clean.
- Can be enjoyed hot or cold.

Gulab jaman

The syrup for gulab jaman can as easily be made using coconut sugar, in which case double the amount of water. Equally rice syrup, maple syrup, agave syrup or even golden syrup from cane sugar is suitable.

Syrup soaked balls of heaven, gulab jaman are an South Asian dessert made of milk powder and wheat flour...our version has taken years to develop to get the same texture and taste explosion...

For the syrup:

> ¼ cup of water
> 1 cup syrup - we use a blend of carob, grape and apple
> 6 green cardamoms
> 1 cinnamon stick
> 1 TBL rose water

- Combine everything in a pan except the rose water and bring it to the boil.
- Remove from the heat.
- When the syrup is just warm and not hot, add the rose water. Set aside.

For the dough:

> 1 cup quinoa, rinsed
> ¼ cup buckwheat flour
> 2 tsp baking powder
> fine zest of ½ orange and ½ lemon
> ¼ cup plant mylk for the dough
> Sunflower oil for deep frying
> ¼ tsp salt

- Cook the quinoa gently in 2 cups of water with the lid off. When the water is absorbed, remove from the heat.
- Combine everything, except for the sunflower oil, in a bowl.
- Form balls, but don't press them together hard or they will come out like bullets.
- Deep fry in the sunflower oil until golden.
- Remove them from the oil and submerge them immediately in the warm syrup.
- Cool outside of the fridge as the shock of sudden change in temperature will cause them to dimple.

Chocolate mousse

It's easy to change this recipe and make a citrus mousse. Leave out the cocoa powder, add the zest of one citrus fruit. Squeeze the juice of the fruit into a calibrated container and then top it up to the 175ml mark. Up the cornflour to 2½ TBL.

By increasing the cornflour to 3 TBL, both the chocolate and the citrus versions will also double as filler for a 'cheese'cake, pouring the mix over a ready base. Cool, cut and serve.

Good cheating bases for gluten-free cheesecakes are: chocolate chips, citrus slices or zest, any sliced fresh fruit, dessicated coconut, maize meal or the 'cheese'cake base on p.194

The ideal vessel for serving this dessert is a parfait glass or a wine glass. The presentation then shows the layers through the glass.

All you need is:

> 300g soft tofu
> ⅓ cup of cocoa
> 2 TBL cornflour
> 175ml soya mylk
> 150ml syrup
> 1 tsp salt
> 2 tsp vanilla
> ½ of a 400ml tin/can coconut milk

- Open the can of coconut milk. Usually the coconut cream has separated from coconut water or 'whey'. Stir the contents and blend them together.
- Whizz everything, except the coconut milk, in a heavy bottomed pan.
- Cook on a medium heat stirring constantly.
- Remove from the heat the minute bubbles appear. An extra whizz now it is cooked will yield a really smooth result.
- Spoon 2 TBL coconut into each glass.
- Divide the warm mix between the glasses, pouring it onto the coconut already at the base.
- Stir the contents of each glass so as to fold the two ingredients together rather than to fully blend them.
- Pour any remaining coconut on the top.
- Refrigerate at least 2 hours before serving.

Sticky toffee pudding

On p.162 there is a lot of chat about being carful when making sugar-free claims that may be false.

No added fat and no added sugar for this dessert in the cake. The sauce is similarly free of added fat or sugar.

Make the pudding by first pre-heating the oven to medium. Oil a 1500 mould.

> *400g dried, stoned dates*
> *375ml rice mylk*
> *80g chickpea flour aka gram, besan or garbanzo bean flour*
> *½ tsp vanilla and ½ tsp salt*
> *1 TBL baking powder*

- *Cook the dates, mylk salt and vanilla in pan on a low heat until the dates are soft*
- *Whizz with the chickpea flour until smooth.*
- *Mix in the baking powder with a hand whisk to ensure even distribution - it can get caught in just one place with a hand blender.*
- *Pour into the mould and then into the oven quickly so that the baking powder is not exhausted.*
- *Bake for 20-30 minutes until the cake is solid to touch and has some spring. Remove.*

Make the toffee sauce:

> *2½ cups of dried, stoned dates*
> *500ml rice mylk*
> *1 tsp vanilla*
> *1 tsp salt*

- *Heat on a low heat until the dates have softened.*
- *Whizz and serve hot over the pudding.*

Universal muffins

Just as the recipe allows for variation in flavour, so too one may vary the flours. Muffins are a great way to experiment with flours such as those made from rice, maize, including polenta, beans and peas. Just see what you prefer. The textures will differ but cupcakes seem to disappear whatever flour we use!

Whether decorated cup cakes with the sweet side played up, or whether muffins that are left plain and full of fresh fruit for a healthier option, this universal recipe can be modified and adapted to your own taste. Makes 12 small muffins.

Pre-heat the oven to medium heat.

3 cups buckwheat flour
1 cup of coconut sugar
1 cup of sunflower oil
2½ cups of coconut mylk drink. (Any mylk will do.)
1 tsp vanilla
½ tsp salt
3 TBL baking powder

- Whisk together the oil, vanilla and coconut sugar.
- Add the mylk.
- Fold in the flour, salt and baking powder.
- Divide between 12 cupcake moulds.
- Bake 15-20 minutes or until they are solid
  to the touch. Remove and set to cool.

Easy variations: flavour with spices and citrus zest, fold in fresh berries or chocolate chips, or both. Go savoury with diced onions and chopped herbs... The muffins freeze readily and transport easily for picnics and packed lunches.

Ice cream

Alice and Bob are the EL PIANO ice-cream makers and but for our neighbour Matt, who gave us his industrial machine, we may never have progressed to such dizzying heights as both soya and coconut varieties.

The following recipe is a base, add more vanilla for Vanilla, add cocoa and more salt for Chocolate. Add fresh mint for Mint. Leave out some of the mylk and add soft fruit for intense fruit flavours... the possibilites are only limited by your imagination.

Whizz together until thick:

> *375ml soya mylk/1 tin coconut milk*
> *125ml sunflower oil*
> *100ml syrup*
> *1 tsp xanthum gum - acts as a thickener and stabiliser*
> *1 tsp vanilla*
> *¼ tsp salt*
> *dash of vodka to help keep it soft - vodka does not freeze. When making an alcoholic flavour, such as rum and raisin ice cream, leave out the vodka as the alcohol, such as rum, will serve the same purpose*

Domestic ice-cream machines:

> *These are inexpensive, do not contain a refrigeration unit but are potentially worth investing in. You do need a large enough freezer space for the bowl. Follow the manufacturer's instructions.*

Small commerical machines:

> *These are fantastic if you are mad on ice-cream. They produce only small amounts but do contain a refrigeration unit which freezes as it churns.*

Stop-gap method:

> *Divide the mix between ice-cube trays and freeze. Turn out the cubes as needed and whizz them with a touch of mylk. It's a bit tough to do so, so you need to persevere as the cubes thaw. Unlike the other methods, when you have this ice-cream it all needs eating and cannot be re-frozen. On the plus side, you need only select the number of cubes you need per event.*

9
Drinks

Granada chai

It's interesting how foods can trace a connection between us. This tea, so often found in Granada, is almost exactly like tea in Pakistan. And think of blumenkohl in German (flower cabbage). Coliflor in Spanish (arguably kohl y flor (flower). Which in English comes out as caul -i- flower... Fun.

The syrup can be kept for weeks in the fridge and used to flavour not only drinks, whether hot or cold, but also sauces.

You will need:

1 TBL crushed green cardamoms
1 TBL crushed coriander seeds
1 fresh red chilli - broken for heat - keep it whole for reduced heat (so the seeds do not escape)
1 cinnamon stick (5cm)
½ tsp nutmeg
250g coconut sugar
5 tea bags of black tea

- Put everything in a pan with 1L of water.
- Bring to the boil and simmer for 5-10 minutes.
- Dilute with mylk, 100ml of chai to 200ml of mylk..

Hot chocolate syrup

This syrup, undiluted, can also be used as a topping for cakes and ice-cream.

You will need:

300ml water
250ml/350g syrup
150g cocoa powder
½ tsp vanilla
½ tsp salt
more sweetener to taste

- Put everything in a pan.
- Heat gently to 85°, in other words less than boiling, as it is easy to burn.
- Dilute: 100ml of chocolate syrup to 200ml of mylk.
- Can be enjoyed hot or cold.

Ginger beer

When we ditched refined sugar, all the carbonated drinks had to go. Bye-bye pop, dandelion and burdock, Victorian lemonade, gingerbeer. And bye-bye all that wretched glass as well, and all the costs of having it hauled and disposed of. Bye-bye excess sugar intake. Hello to Elena, Alice and Bob's alternatives... and welcome to any commercial operator wishing to use them. The business case is super strong, sales are unaffected and waste is reduced.

There are two options here: instant gratification and fermentation with potential excitement...

For an instant result, make the ginger base:

> 1 part ginger juice (squeezed out of fresh ginger root)
> 1 part lemon juice
> 1 part syrup
> 1 part water

- *Make the ginger beer with 1 part base and 2 parts carbonated water.*
- *Serve.*

For fermentation, with the potential of excitement:

> a preparation of warmed ginger base, exactly as above
> a few granules of champagne yeast - 30 granules per 1L of base

- *Combine the base with the yeast and put in a sealed container.*
- *Store in a warm place for 48 hours.*
- *Transfer to the refrigerator for a further 24 hours. This is essential as it halts the fermentation process.*
- *Serve.*

Excitement can result from highly fermented ginger, which one cannot predict, and fizzed fermented fluid spilling over...

Fizz

Make the cordial:

> 2 parts crushed fruits or fresh juice
> 1 part syrup

- *Mix 1 part cordial with 2 parts carbonated water.*
- *Stir and serve.*

Variations are: mint and lemon; replacing some of the juice in the cordial with cold berry tea.

Rock 'n' rye

Creating your own family recipe book is a worthy project. Noting not only the recipes you have liked and tweaked to your own taste, but also remembering family, their kitchen triumphs and disasters. One of the joys of EL PIANO has been bringing our family recipes to the menu. The passing on of recipes is arguably the last great oral tradition in the West.

Bob's great-grandmother MynSue was born on the American frontier in 1899. She and her sister Dorcas, (born February 29, 1896 and not having a birthday therefore until 1904 when she was 8 years old), kept a still for a while producing rye whiskey. In common with all their neighbours, it was rough as guts. This recipe was their remedy. From October onwards, even as very elderly women, the daily cry from MynSue to Dorcas, or vice versa, was: "Say, Sister! Do you think the rock 'n' rye is ready yet?"

You will need:

> 1 bottle of nasty rye whiskey
> 1 string of rock candy or 40g of similar seaside rock
> - mint flavoured will work, but plain is better
> 1 cinnamon stick
> 10 dried sour cherries
> 2 months, ideally October and November

- Decant the rye into a clear glass bottle or decanter so you can see what is going on week by week.
- Drop in the rock candy, cinnamon and cherries.
- Leave the liquor 2 months or until the candy is disssolved.
- Drink with caution.

Cowboy coffee

This is our last recipe, and we end where EL PIANO began: cowboy coffee. Long before we had a fully fledged restaurant we served this coffee. It's been on the menu since 1997, longer than the dhal on p.128. Before we opened we even served it to the workmen who kitted out the eatery. It's the simplest thing to make and among the most deeply satisfying. Magdalena's father made it on the campfire as a young cowboy. It kept him awake on the long ride, kept him sharp while he sucked the poison out of a rattlesnake bite, and, as he used to say, kept him 'regular' on the trail...

You will need:

> ground coffee beans that are blond and strong
> a jug, a strainer and boiling water

- Spoon 2 TBL of coffee per person into the jug.
- Pour on the hot water. Stir once.
- Let the grounds fall in their own time.
- Then sieve and enjoy.

Rolling sausages...

- Put a roll of cling film or 'saran' wrap behind a flat chopping board so that it's easy to roll out directly onto the board.

- Lay a long sausage of mix along the plastic from left to right. Leave the edge of the film nearest to you free.

- Pull on the film, wrap it over the sausage. Roll it on the board to enclose it. Run a knife across the film on the board to separate it from the roll.

- Seal the ends by pressing them down. Now they are ready to steam.

Coconut

We use six sorts of coconut in our recipes and refer to them as:

- **creamed coconut** - sold as a solid block, packed in carboard, usually 200g, which we have sourced free from sulphur dioxide.
- **coconut milk** - sold in tins or cans and extremely variable in both quality, often grainy and grey, and in the proportion of cream.
- **coconut cream** - this is the same product as coconut milk, above, but refers to the solid coconut fat in the tins of coconut milk. In some of our recipes we only use the solid part of each tin. The more watery part, or the 'whey' can be used in drinks, curries or soups.
- **coconut mylk drink** - sold in 1L tetrapaks, with no noticeable coconut flavour, used instead of dairy milk or other plant mylks.
- **coconut oil** - sold as solid fat in jars and often used in place of butter.
- **dessicated coconut** - this is dried coconut in flakes of varying sizes. We use finely flaked.

Sweeteners

Not using refined sugar in EL PIANO, and eliminating cane sugar, does not mean that there is no sugar in our food. Arguably, syrups are refined anyway, in that they all go through a cleansing or heating process. However, different sources of sweetness do have a less detrimental impact on health. This is by no means a comprehensive list of what is available. These are merely the sweeteners that we use in EL PIANO.

- agave syrup
- apple juice concentrate
- apple syrup
- carob syrup
- coconut sugar aka coconut nectar
- date syrup
- jaggery
- maple syrup
- rice syrup

Sweeteners can be avoided altogether in some recipes by introducing vanilla and cinnamon. Somehow those flavours in pancakes, cakes and biscuits can fool us into experiencing sweet sensations.

Index of allergens

Of the fourteen officially recognised allergens, EL PIANO uses five. These are: **celery**, **sesame**, **soya**, **sulphites**, **mustard**. Of more than 150 recipes in the book, only 18 call for any of the official allergens. Please double check the ingredients list of each recipe. We have been able to source creamed coconut that is free of sulphur dioxide, but take care when you buy as many are not. Most of our wines are organic and some are free from or low in sulphites.

Recipe	Page	Allergen it contains
Hummus	16	Sesame
Lawrence's pâte	20	Soya
Sweet potato mousse	24	Soya
Scotch egg	50	Soya
Waldorf salad	70	Soya
Potato salad	76	Soya and mustard
Sweet & sour tofu	90	Soya - can be made without tofu
Kofta	94	Soya
Chilli	100	Soya
Clever quiche - spinach	104	Soya - only in the pastry case
Pan fried tofu	120	Soya
Thai duo	122	Soya - can be made without tofu
Keema Mathar	134	Soya
Satay skewers	140	Soya
Mexi duo	144	Soya - only in the garnish
Rhaita	156	Soya
Mayo	158	Soya
Chocolate mousse	202	Soya

Our Madras curry powder contains mustard but there are plenty of blends that do not. Be aware that poorer quality ground spices may contain hidden wheat flour as a filler to help reduce prices. Seek out reputable suppliers.

Key suppliers

A restaurant is only as good as its suppliers.

Abundance - *abundance@edibleyork.org*
each year these guys provide us with local fruits for our chutneys.

Barnitts - *barnitts.co.uk*
ironmongers extraordinaire. It's a well known truth that every breakdown in eateries happens between 5pm on a Friday and 9am on a Monday.

Brass Castle Brewery - *brasscastle.co.uk*
local gluten free beers from Malton just for us!!! (Well, and others too!)

Carroll's Heritage Potatoes - *heritage-potatoes.co.uk*
a huge range of organic, heritage potatoes. They will ship to you directly from their farm.

Hodmedod - *www.hodmedod.co.uk*
their trials in growing quinoa have made it possible for us to incorporate it into our menu. They offer their products online in domestic sizes, see p. 195.

Lembas Foods - *lembas.co.uk*
great organic and vegan products at great prices. They offer home delivery.

David Miller - *millerfoodservice.co.uk*
efficient, frequent, uncomplicated food service.

Simon Baynes - *simonbaynes.net*
our fruit and veg merchant for more than 20 years. 'Nuff said. See Simon on p.60.

Sweet Freedom - *sweetfreedom.co.uk*
blended syrups and sweetener alternatives to cane sugar.

Ward's of York - *wardscatering.co.uk*
catering equipment suppliers. You may travel the country, but we are glad you are here.

Yorkshire Orchards - *yorkshireorchards.co.uk*
the only fruit juice we buy in. Local fruits and blends.

Country Products and Field & Fawcett Wines each extended us such a long line of credit when we were younger. Thank you both. And Tullivers for always being great in a snip. In over 20 years of trading we have plenty of suppliers to be thankful for.

Then there are the master builders - Nigel Bone, Matthias Garn, Mal Pavis, Damian Doherty, Paul Reeder. See their amazing work on our conservation grade building.

Last, but by NO means least, the professionals - Bill and Liz Chadwick, Kevin Grant, Barry Crux, Jon Steel - there are no words for the excellence of supply.

a founder's last words...

Sticky stuff won't stick to wet hands.

Pay proper money for good advisors and then take their advice.

Cook everything in domestic-sized batches.

Beware landlords bearing gifts.

No-one is always right, and customers are no exception.

Pay all staff above minimum wage, right from the start.

Don't lie to the government. In fact, it's probably best not to lie to anyone.

Change the oil in the fryers daily.

Don't employ people who don't need the money.

What will you choose? Buy organic local ingredients or matching cutlery?

Look at the sales monthly, not daily.

Celebrate every triumph, no matter how small.

We can make our own small world of a restaurant a better place.

The standard models of business are not necessarily the right ones.

Kindness counts. Respect is fundamental.

The perfect is the enemy of the good.

Ask yourself, 'What can I do to make my customers' experience better this year?'

Assume good-will.

'You can sleep when you're dead' needs modifying. Sleep is important.

Put others equal to yourself, except for wages – always pay the staff first.

Make an annual fantasy shopping list.

Never write an email in a state of high emotion.

The price of a meal does not buy the right to abuse those who serve it.

Kitchen notes

Kitchen notes

Kitchen notes